Good Housekeeping

Best
Italian Recipes

Delicious Pastas, Breads, Desserts & Main Dishes

HEARST BOOKS
A division of Sterling Publishing Co., Inc.

New York / London
www.sterlingpublishing.com

Originally published by Hearst Books in a different format as *Good Housekeeping 100 Best Italian Recipes*

Supplemental text by Brenda Goldberg
Book design by Richard Oriolo

Photography Credits

FRONT COVER Mark Thomas

BACK COVER Brian Hagiwara (left and center), Rita Maas (right)

INTERIOR

Brian Hagiwara 27, 47, 51, 52, 53

Rita Maas 9, 69 (top), 81, 82, 90

Steven Mark Needham 127

Alan Richardson 12, 69 (bottom)

Ann Stratton spine, 15, 21, 55, 84, 101, 103, 120, 133, 137, 138, 153, 154, 155

Mark Thomas 29, 31, 34, 36, 62, 123, 125

The Good Housekeeping Seal guarantees that the recipes in this cookbook meet the strict standards of the Good Housekeeping Research Institute. The Institute has been a source of reliable information and a consumer advocate since 1900, and established its seal of approval in 1909. Every recipe has been triple-tested for ease, reliability, and great taste.

Hearst Books
A division of Sterling Publishing Co., Inc.
387 Park Avenue South
New York, NY 10016

Good Housekeeping is a registered trademark of Hearst Communications, Inc.

www.goodhousekeeping.com

Manufactured in China
ISBN 978-1-58816-880-1

10 9 8 7 6 5 4 3 2 1

Contents

Foreword

Growing up in an Italian-American family, I spent a lot of time around the dinner table. Sunday dinners at my grandparents' house meant many courses and several hours of leisurely eating and talking at the table. It wasn't until I spent time in Italy that I realized just what my grandparents had preserved for us. My first glimpse was at my great-uncle's table near Rome, when as a college student, I watched him peel a pear with a knife and fork. I was transported back to my 4-year old self, in awe of my grandfather, seated at the head of the table, perfectly peeling a pear with his knife and fork.

My grandfather owned a produce store and he prided himself on being able to choose the best of everything. So there were always lots of fresh vegetables on our table, served with a drizzle of olive oil, which I'm sure wasn't extravirgin back then. For everyday meals, my mother's food, whether a minestrone, pasta, or roast pork, was simple, delicious, and abundant.

Perhaps it's the memory of that ever present decanter at my grandfathers' elbow that makes me love big red wines, but they do go well with many dishes in this book. For meat or tomato-based dishes try a Barbera, Chianti, or Primitivo from Italy. California winemakers have adopted some Italian varietals and there are great choices and values much like their old country originals: Barbera, Zinfandel (similar to Primitivo), and Sangiovese (the grape of Chianti). For lovers of white wines, match seafood, poultry and light appetizers with Pinot Grigio, Soave, or Orvieto. Prosecco, the delicious sparkling wine from the Veneto makes a perfect *apertivo*.

Life at the table, among friends and family is a ritual that is central to Italian culture. There is a sense of togetherness that makes any meal a celebration. I hope that the recipes in this book will inspire you to gather friends and family at your table for dinner Italian-style. Savor the food—and your enjoyment of one another.

—Susan Westmoreland
FOOD DIRECTOR, *Good Housekeeping*

Introduction

LA CUCINA ITALIANA

Ask Americans what their favorite ethnic food is, and the majority will answer, "Italian." No longer just spaghetti and meatballs and pizza—still the standard bearers—Italian cuisine in America has expanded to include such traditional staples as rice, polenta, and myriad colorful, flavor-packed Mediterranean vegetables.

WHAT MAKES ITALIAN FOOD ITALIAN? In Italy, the best dishes are not just for guests but are lavished on the family, too. In keeping with this tradition, home cooks demand top-quality food products. And in Italy quality means freshness and flavor. Whatever the method of preparation, cooks strive only to enhance, never transform, what nature has already provided. It's this respect for the ingredients that makes Italian food so special—and so popular.

THE ITALIAN LARDER

Certain products are very specific to Italian cuisine.

OLIVE OIL Used in Mediterranean cooking since antiquity, olive oil is fundamental to Italian cuisine where it is used as both a condiment and cooking medium. Extravirgin olive oil is obtained from fresh green or ripe olives and is minimally treated. Of the highest quality and price, its flavor, color, and fragrance depend on the source of the olives and condition of the harvest, so taste can vary not only from brand to brand but from year to year. Its luscious fruity flavor and aromatic bouquet make it ideal for drizzling as a finishing touch to uncooked dishes and over salads, for adding to soups and stews at table, and for dipping bread. It is generally not used for cooking. The familiar light golden olive oil (what we used to call "pure") is a processed oil that undergoes additional filtration. It has a mild, but still distinctive olive flavor. It is a good everyday oil for sautéeing and deep-frying. By definition a highly processed oil, "light" olive oil refers to its flavor, which has little, if any, olive taste, rather than its calorie or fat content. All olive oil has the same amount of calories.

Once opened, olive oil can be stored in a cool dark place for up to six months. Don't buy more than you can use as it can turn rancid, especially if stored in a warm place.

BALSAMIC VINEGAR The process for making balsamic vinegar, cooking and aging fresh grape must (juice), has been handed down from generation to generation since the 11th century. Artisanal balsamic is famous for its syrupy consistency and sweet tangy flavor, which is accomplished by aging in several varieties of progressively smaller wooden barrels, not by adding sweeteners. The oldest of these vinegars, by law at least 12 years, are called *tradizionale* and are reserved for drizzling on meat or berries, or even served after dinner as a digestive.

Commercial balsamic vinegar does not have to be aged and often consists of a small amount of artisanal vinegar mixed with wine vinegar and caramel color. Artisanal or commercial balsamics are fine for the recipes in this book. All balsamic vinegars can be stored indefinitely at room temperature in a cool dark place.

CHEESE Italian cheese is not just about Parmesan and mozzarella.

- Gorgonzola is Italy's beloved blue cheese. Rich, firm, and pungent, it is delicious with fruit or crumbled over a salad. It is also used to make rich sauces, such as in our Farfalle with Gorgonzola Sauce (page 57).
- Mozzarella is a pure white semisoft cheese with a mild, almost sweet flavor that is prized for its melting qualities. Once made from the milk of water buffalo, it is made mainly from cow's milk nowadays. Americans know mozzarella as a pizza topping, but it is also used sliced in sandwiches and other dishes.
- Parmesan is Italy's most popular grating cheese. It is pale straw-yellow with a very hard yellow-brown rind and will last indefinitely. Aged Parmesan is dry and granular and tastes best when freshly grated. The finest Parmesan is stamped *Parmigiano-Reggiano* on its rind and comes from the area around Parma.
- Pecorino Romano, made from sheeps milk, is the favorite grating cheese of Rome and Southern Italy. It's salty, tangy flavor makes it a perfect partner to hearty tomato sauces.
- Ricotta is a soft white fresh cheese similar to cottage cheese that is available as a whole- or skimmed-milk product. It is used as a filling in sweet and savory dishes as well as desserts.

- Ricotta salata is no relation to soft ricotta. It is a pressed lightly salted Sicilian sheep's milk cheese with a slightly crumbly, firm texture. Delicious as an eating cheese, it also tops many Southern pasta dishes.

VEGETABLES Italy would not be Italy without its markets, where a panoply of fresh-picked vegetables lure cooks on a daily basis.

Artichokes: A relative of the thistle and a Mediterranean native, Italian cooks steam, stuff, sauté, and even deep fry them. Try Braised Baby Artichokes with Olives (page 10) for a lovely appetizer.

Arugula: A member of the cabbage family, arugula is related to watercress, mustard, and radishes. Also know as rocket, it is a pungent, peppery salad green with long, slender, lobed leaves.

Broccoli rabe: Also known as broccoli raab, rabe, and *broccoli di rape*, broccoli rabe does not taste like broccoli. It is a sharp-flavored green of the cabbage family with long edible stems, narrow leaves, and small bud clusters. Italian cooks bring out its sweetness by blanching it in boiling water first, then sautéeing it in olive oil with a bit of garlic or with sausage.

Eggplant: Although we think of eggplant as a vegetable, it is really the fruit of a plant that originated in India. The most common variety is the deep purple oval one that resembles a pear. The skin is edible, but some varieties have very bitter skins, so it is best to peel it.

Escarole: Used by the Greeks and Romans for its medicinal properties, escarole has been consumed as a vegetable since the 14th century. In Italy, escarole is used in soups and salads or served as a side dish.

Fennel: Also know as *finocchio*, Florence fennel, or anise, this vegetable is a Mediterranean favorite. It resembles a flattened bunch of celery with a bulbous white base, long pale green stalks, and feathery green leaves. It has a distinctive yet subtle licorice taste. Thinly slice it and use raw in salads or braise or roast it to bring out its sweetness. Generally available from late fall through early spring, it does not keep well, so buy it just before you intend to use it.

Zucchini: To Americans, zucchini is probably the most familiar summer squash. Some mistake its very delicate taste for blandness and end up obliterating it with heavy seasoning. In Italy, however, cooks take care to bring out its distinct yet subtle flavor. For best results, only buy zucchini that are no longer than 6 to 8 inches and no thicker than 1½ inches in diameter. They should feel firm, not flabby. Be sure not to overcook them.

PASTA The Chinese may have invented pasta, but Italians have made it a versatile medium with which to work culinary magic. In this book, we use dried Italian-style pasta, which is available everywhere and easy to turn into a quick meal. For creamy or light-bodied sauces, homemade or prepared fresh pasta is also an excellent choice. Made with eggs, fresh pasta has a silky surface and a delicate texture. Dried pasta, made from flour and water, is more economical, lower in fat, and a good match for robust, strong-flavored sauces.

For the best taste and texture, buy dried pasta made from durum wheat flour or from semolina flour. Store dried pasta in a cool, dry, dark place for up to one year and whole-wheat pasta for up to six months. Don't store pasta in clear containers: Exposing it to light destroys riboflavin, a key nutrient in pasta. Buy pasta in cardboard boxes, which keep out light, rather than in clear packaging.

Store commercially made fresh pasta in the refrigerator according to the package directions for up to one week, or freeze for up to one month. For the best results, don't thaw frozen pasta before cooking.

RICE Arborio, Carnaroli, and Vialone Nano are all types of short-, round-grained rice grown in northern Italy. Depending upon the locale, one of these is used to prepare risotto, a dish that has become a regular on Italian restaurant menus. The traditional method of preparing risotto is not complicated, but it does require a bit of time. The goal is to make the rice absorb enough hot broth until it swells and turns into a mass of creamy, yet still slightly firm grains.

POLENTA Polenta is another word for cornmeal. There are two types: finely ground and coarsely ground. Which one you use is simply a matter of personal preference. However, coarsely ground polenta will have a more interesting texture. Creamy Polenta (page 75) is simple to prepare.

BEANS When fresh beans are not available, most Italian cooks will use dried beans. Dried beans keep for about one year, but they become less flavorful and drier as time passes, and older beans take longer to cook. Beans are not stamped with a "sell-by" date, so purchase them from a grocer with high turnover.

Canned beans are a boon to the busy cook because they don't require soaking or further cooking, and some people find them easier to digest than freshly cooked dried beans. Different brands vary greatly in texture and saltiness, however, so take note of your favorite label. Canned beans should be rinsed and drained under cold water before being used. This quick rinse refreshes their flavor and removes some of the sodium added during the canning process.

Appetizers
& Soups

Tomato and Ricotta Salata Bruschetta (page 16)
and Tuscan White-Bean Bruschetta (page 18)

Braised Baby Artichokes with Olives

An inspired way to cook baby artichokes—accented with garlic and olives.

PREP 20 minutes **COOK** 15 minutes **MAKES** 8 first-course servings.

2 pounds baby artichokes (about 16)

1 lemon, cut in half

$^1/_4$ cup olive oil

3 garlic cloves, sliced

1 cup water

$^1/_2$ teaspoon salt

$^1/_2$ teaspoon coarsely ground black pepper

$^1/_3$ cup oil-cured olives, pitted and coarsely chopped

1. Trim artichokes: Bend back outer green leaves and snap off at base until remaining leaves are green on top and yellow on bottom. Cut off stems level with bottom of artichoke. Cut off top half of each artichoke and discard. Rub cut surfaces with lemon to prevent browning. Cut each artichoke lengthwise in half or into quarters if large, dropping them into bowl of cold water and juice of remaining lemon half.

2. In nonstick 12-inch skillet, heat *1 inch water* to boiling over high heat. Drain artichokes and add to skillet; cook 5 minutes. Drain. Wipe skillet dry with paper towels.

3. In same skillet, heat oil over medium-high heat. Add garlic and cook until golden. Add artichokes; cook until lightly browned, about 2 minutes. Stir in water, salt, and pepper; cover and cook until knife inserted in bottom of artichoke goes in easily, about 5 minutes longer. Stir in olives and heat through.

EACH SERVING About 103 calories | 2g protein | 6g carbohydrate | 9g total fat (1g saturated) | 0mg cholesterol | 383mg sodium.

Marinated Mixed Olives

Here, an assortment of olives is marinated in extravirgin olive oil and seasoned with garlic, fennel, bay leaves, and lemon. Keep a supply on hand for a last-minute appetizer.

PREP 10 minutes plus standing and marinating   **COOK** 5 minutes
MAKES about 6 cups.

$^1/_4$ **cup extravirgin olive oil**

2 teaspoons fennel seeds, crushed

4 small bay leaves

2 pounds assorted Mediterranean olives, such as Niçoise, picholine, or Kalamata

6 strips (3" by 1" each) lemon peel

4 garlic cloves, crushed with side of chef's knife

1. In 1-quart saucepan, heat oil, fennel seeds, and bay leaves over medium heat until hot but not smoking. Remove saucepan from heat; let stand 10 minutes.

2. In large bowl, combine olives, lemon peel, garlic, and oil mixture. Cover and refrigerate, stirring occasionally, at least 24 hours or up to several days to blend flavors.

3. Store in refrigerator up to 1 month. Discard bay leaves and drain to serve.

EACH $^1/_4$ **CUP** About 107 calories | 1g protein | 3g carbohydrate | 10g total fat (1g saturated) | 0mg cholesterol | 680mg sodium.

Roasted Prosciutto-Wrapped Asparagus

Perfect for a dinner party appetizer—you can oven-steam the asparagus in advance, then roast the wrapped spears just before serving. The recipe works best with medium-size asparagus spears because they're easier to handle as finger food.

PREP 30 minutes **STEAM/ROAST** 20 minutes
MAKES 12 first-course servings or 24 appetizers.

24 medium asparagus spears
(about 1 1/2 pounds), trimmed

12 thin slices prosciutto
(about 8 ounces), each cut
lengthwise in half

1/2 cup freshly grated Parmesan
cheese

1. Preheat oven to 400°F. Place asparagus and *¼ cup boiling water* in large roasting pan (17" by 11½"); cover pan with foil. Place in oven and let steam until tender, 10 to 15 minutes. Transfer asparagus to paper towels to drain; pat dry. Wipe pan dry.

2. On waxed paper, place 1 prosciutto strip; sprinkle with 1 teaspoon Parmesan. Place asparagus spear on end of prosciutto strip. Roll the prosciutto around asparagus spear, slightly overlapping prosciutto as you roll to cover most of spear. Repeat with remaining asparagus, prosciutto, and Parmesan.

3. Place wrapped asparagus in roasting pan (it's all right if spears touch) and roast until asparagus is heated through and prosciutto just begins to brown, about 10 minutes.

EACH FIRST-COURSE SERVING About 50 calories | 7g protein | 1g carbohydrate | 2g total fat (1g saturated) | 15mg cholesterol | 540mg sodium.

Black Forest Ham-Wrapped Asparagus

Prepare as directed, but substitute **12 thin slices Black Forest ham** (about 8 ounces) for prosciutto and **1 cup shredded Gruyère cheese** (about 1½ teaspoons per spear) for Parmesan.

EACH FIRST-COURSE SERVING About 80 calories | 8g protein | 1g carbohydrate | 5g total fat (2g saturated) | 21mg cholesterol | 315mg sodium.

Lacy Parmesan Crisps

Called *frico* in Italy, these delicious wafers are simply spoonfuls of grated cheese that are baked and cooled. Reusable nonstick bakeware liners, available at most kitchenware stores and bakery suppliers, give the best results and are easy to use, but you can use a nonstick cookie sheet or nonstick foil instead.

PREP 20 minutes **BAKE** 6 minutes per batch **MAKES** about 24 crisps.

6 ounces Parmesan cheese, coarsely grated (1^1/$_2$ cups)

1. Preheat oven to 375°F. Line large cookie sheet with reusable nonstick bakeware liner. Drop level tablespoons of Parmesan 3 inches apart onto cookie sheet; spread to form 2-inch rounds.

2. Bake Parmesan rounds until edges just begin to color, 6 to 7 minutes. Transfer crisps, still on bakeware liner, to wire rack; cool 2 minutes. Transfer to paper towels to drain. Repeat with remaining Parmesan.

EACH CRISP About 28 calories | 3g protein | 0g carbohydrate | 2g total fat (1g saturated) | 5mg cholesterol | 114mg sodium.

Tomato and Ricotta Salata Bruschetta

Bruschetta is toasted Italian bread that is rubbed with garlic and drizzled with olive oil. It's often topped with savory ingredients to make a simple appetizer. Here, we use ripe tomatoes and ricotta salata, a lightly salted pressed sheep's milk cheese. Ricotta salata can be found at Italian markets and specialty food stores (see photo on page 9).

PREP 25 minutes **BAKE** 5 minutes **MAKES** 16 bruschetta.

1 loaf (8 ounces) Italian bread, cut on diagonal into $1/2$-inch-thick slices

8 garlic cloves, each cut in half

1 pound ripe plum tomatoes (6 medium), seeded and cut into $1/2$-inch pieces

1 tablespoon finely chopped red onion

1 tablespoon chopped fresh basil

4 ounces ricotta salata, feta, or goat cheese, cut into $1/2$-inch pieces

2 tablespoons extravirgin olive oil

2 teaspoons balsamic vinegar

$1/4$ teaspoon salt

$1/4$ teaspoon coarsely ground black pepper

1. Preheat oven to 400°F. Place bread slices on cookie sheet and bake until lightly toasted, about 5 minutes. Rub one side of each toast slice with cut side of garlic.

2. Meanwhile, in bowl, gently toss tomatoes, onion, basil, cheese, oil, vinegar, salt, and pepper until combined.

3. To serve, spoon tomato mixture on garlic-rubbed side of toast slices.

EACH BRUSCHETTA About 79 calories | 2g protein | 9g carbohydrate | 4g total fat (1g saturated) | 6mg cholesterol | 236mg sodium.

Bruschetta with Tomatoes, Basil, and Olives

A classic Mediterranean mix of herbs, tomatoes, and olives on toasted French or Italian bread makes a nice nibble when you serve cocktails.

PREP 20 minutes **BROIL** 2 minutes **MAKES** about 16 bruschetta.

1 loaf (8 ounces) French or Italian bread, cut on diagonal into $1/2$-inch-thick slices

1 garlic clove, peeled and cut in half

8 ripe small tomatoes (about $1^1/2$ pounds), chopped

$1/4$ cup Kalamata olives, pitted and chopped

$1/4$ cup loosely packed fresh basil leaves, chopped

$1/4$ cup loosely packed fresh parsley leaves, chopped

3 tablespoons extravirgin olive oil

$1/4$ teaspoon salt

$1/8$ teaspoon coarsely ground black pepper

1. Preheat broiler. Place bread slices in $15^1/2$" by $10^1/2$" jelly-roll pan. Place pan in broiler at closest position to heat source. Broil bread until lightly toasted, about 1 minute per side. Rub one side of each toast slice with cut side of garlic.

2. In medium bowl, gently toss tomatoes, olives, basil, parsley, oil, salt, and pepper until combined.

3. To serve, spoon tomato mixture on garlic-rubbed side of toast slices.

EACH BRUSCHETTA About 70 calories | 1g protein | 9g carbohydrate | 4g total fat (1g saturated) | 0mg cholesterol | 145mg sodium.

Tuscan White-Bean Bruschetta

A first course made with slices of grilled bread and classic Tuscan-style beans—the perfect way to begin an outdoor dinner cooked on the grill (see photo on page 9).

PREP 15 minutes **GRILL** 10 minutes **MAKES** 16 bruschetta.

1 loaf (8 ounces) Italian bread, cut on diagonal into $^1/_2$-inch-thick slices

1 can (15$^1/_2$ to 19 ounces) white kidney beans (cannellini), rinsed and drained

1 tablespoon lemon juice

1 teaspoon minced fresh sage leaves

$^1/_4$ teaspoon salt

$^1/_8$ teaspoon coarsely ground black pepper

3 tablespoons olive oil

3 teaspoons minced fresh parsley leaves

2 garlic cloves, each cut in half

1. Prepare grill.

2. In medium bowl, with fork, lightly mash beans, lemon juice, sage, salt, pepper, 1 tablespoon olive oil, and 2 teaspoons parsley.

3. Place bread slices on grill rack over medium heat and grill until lightly toasted, 3 to 5 minutes on each side. Rub one side of each toast slice with cut side of garlic. Brush with remaining olive oil.

4. To serve, spoon bean mixture on garlic-rubbed side of toast slices and sprinkle with remaining 1 teaspoon parsley.

EACH BRUSCHETTA About 85 calories | 3g protein | 11g carbohydrate | 3g total fat (0g saturated) | 0mg cholesterol | 175mg sodium.

Tuscan Pappa al Pomodoro

The bread acts as the thickener for this comforting Italian tomato soup. It's a cinch to prepare!

PREP 35 minutes plus standing   COOK 15 minutes
MAKES about 10 cups or 10 first-course servings.

1 loaf (8 ounces) several-days-old Tuscan or other country-style bread

3 $^1/_2$ pounds ripe tomatoes

4 garlic cloves, minced

1 teaspoon salt

$^1/_2$ cup extravirgin olive oil

$^1/_2$ teaspoon coarsely ground black pepper

1 can (14$^1/_2$ ounces) chicken or vegetable broth

3 cups water

$^1/_3$ cup minced fresh parsley leaves

$^1/_3$ cup thinly sliced fresh basil leaves

1. Cut bread into 1-inch cubes; place on wire racks to dry, about 1 hour.

2. Meanwhile, peel, seed, and chop tomatoes; set aside. On cutting board, with side of chef's knife, mash garlic with salt to form a smooth paste.

3. In 5-quart Dutch oven, heat oil over low heat. Add garlic paste and cook, stirring, 2 minutes. Stir in bread cubes and pepper and cook, stirring, 2 minutes. Add tomatoes and cook, stirring, 2 minutes longer.

4. Stir in broth and water; heat to boiling over high heat. Remove Dutch oven from heat; cover and let stand 1 hour for flavors to blend.

5. Stir or whisk vigorously until bread is broken up and mixture is almost smooth. Serve soup warm or reheat to serve hot. Just before serving, stir in parsley and basil.

EACH SERVING About 200 calories | 4g protein | 19g carbohydrate | 12g total fat (2g saturated) | 0mg cholesterol | 495mg sodium.

Minestrone with Pesto

Freshly made pesto adds body and richness to this soup.

PREP 20 minutes plus soaking beans **COOK** 1 hour
MAKES about 13 cups or 6 main-dish servings.

8 ounces dry Great Northern beans
(1 1/3 cups), soaked and drained

2 tablespoons olive oil

3 carrots, peeled and cut into
1/4-inch-thick slices

2 stalks celery, cut into
1/4-inch-thick slices

1 large onion (12 ounces),
finely chopped

2 ounces pancetta or bacon,
finely chopped

1 pound all-purpose potatoes
(3 medium), peeled and chopped

2 medium zucchini (8 ounces each),
each cut lengthwise into quarters,
then crosswise into 1/4-inch-thick
slices

1/2 medium head savoy cabbage
(1 pound), thinly sliced

1 large garlic clove, crushed with
garlic press

1 can (14 1/2 ounces) diced tomatoes

2 cans (14 1/2 ounces each) chicken
broth

1 cup water

Pesto (page 22) or 1/2 cup store-
bought pesto

1/2 teaspoon salt

1. In 4-quart saucepan, combine beans and enough *water* to cover by 2 inches; heat to boiling over high heat. Reduce heat; cover and simmer, stirring occasionally, until beans are tender, 40 minutes to 1 hour. Drain beans.

2. Meanwhile, in nonreactive 5-quart Dutch oven, heat oil over medium-high heat. Add carrots, celery, onion, and pancetta; cook, stirring occasionally, until onion begins to brown, about 10 minutes. Add potatoes, zucchini, cabbage, and garlic; cook, stirring constantly, until cabbage has wilted. Add tomatoes with their juice, broth, and water; heat to boiling over high heat. Reduce heat; cover and simmer until vegetables are tender, about 30 minutes.

3. Meanwhile, prepare pesto.

4. In blender or in food processor with knife blade attached, puree $1/2$ cup beans with 1 cup soup mixture until smooth. Stir puree, remaining beans, and salt into soup; heat to boiling. Reduce heat; cover and simmer 10 minutes. Garnish with dollops of pesto.

Pesto

In blender, puree $^2/_3$ cup packed fresh basil leaves, $^1/_4$ cup freshly grated Parmesan cheese, $^1/_4$ cup olive oil, 1 tablespoon water, and $^1/_4$ teaspoon salt until smooth.

EACH SERVING WITH PESTO About 444 calories | 18g protein | 53g carbohydrate | 20g total fat (4g saturated) | 9mg cholesterol | 1,204mg sodium.

Italian White Bean and Spinach Soup

A touch of fresh lemon juice, stirred in just before serving, gives this robust soup a light citrus note.

PREP 20 minutes   **COOK** 30 minutes
MAKES about $7^{1}/_{2}$ cups or 6 first-course servings.

1 tablespoon vegetable oil

1 medium onion, chopped

1 stalk celery, chopped

1 garlic clove, finely chopped

2 cans (15 to 19 ounces each) white kidney beans (cannellini), rinsed and drained

2 cups water

1 can ($14^{1}/_{2}$ ounces) chicken broth

$^{1}/_{4}$ teaspoon coarsely ground black pepper

$^{1}/_{8}$ teaspoon dried thyme

1 bunch (10 to 12 ounces) spinach, tough stems trimmed

1 tablespoon fresh lemon juice

freshly grated Parmesan cheese (optional)

1. In 3-quart saucepan, heat oil over medium heat. Add onion and celery; cook, stirring, until celery is tender, 5 to 8 minutes. Stir in garlic and cook 30 seconds. Add beans, water, broth, pepper, and thyme; heat to boiling over high heat. Reduce heat and simmer 15 minutes.

2. Roll up several spinach leaves together, cigar fashion, and thinly slice. Repeat with remaining spinach.

3. With slotted spoon, remove 2 cups beans from soup mixture and reserve. Spoon one-fourth of mixture into blender; cover, with center part of cover removed to let steam escape, and puree until smooth. Pour into bowl. Repeat with remaining mixture.

4. Return puree and reserved beans to saucepan; heat to boiling over medium-high heat. Stir in spinach and cook just until wilted, about 1 minute. Remove from heat and stir in lemon juice. Serve with Parmesan, if you like.

EACH SERVING About 170 calories | 11g protein | 24g carbohydrate | 4g total fat (1g saturated) | 0mg cholesterol | 539mg sodium.

Chicken and Escarole Soup with Meatballs

Rita Pacella of Brooklyn, grandmother of Gina Miraglia, *Good Housekeeping* friend and recipe developer, makes this soup every year on Thanksgiving. All the grandchildren help roll the tender meatballs—everyone's favorite part.

PREP I hour **COOK** I hour 15 minutes
MAKES about 16 cups or 14 first-course servings.

- I chicken (4 pounds), cut into 8 pieces
- I large onion (12 ounces), cut in half
- $1/4$ teaspoon whole black peppercorns
- I bay leaf
- 12 cups water
- I pound ground meat for meat loaf (beef, pork, and veal)
- 2 garlic cloves, crushed with garlic press
- I large egg, beaten
- $1/4$ cup chopped fresh parsley leaves
- $1/2$ teaspoon coarsely ground black pepper
- $3/4$ cup grated Romano cheese, plus additional for serving
- $2^3/4$ teaspoons salt
- I cup plain dried bread crumbs
- $1/3$ cup milk
- I can ($14^1/2$ ounces) chicken broth
- 3 medium carrots, peeled and sliced
- 2 medium stalks celery, sliced
- I small head escarole (about 8 ounces), cut into $1/2$-inch-wide strips, with tough stems discarded

1. In 8-quart saucepot, combine chicken, onion, peppercorns, bay leaf, and water; heat to boiling over high heat. Reduce heat to low; cover and simmer until chicken is tender, about 1 hour and 15 minutes.

2. Meanwhile, prepare meatballs: In large bowl, with hands, combine ground meat, garlic, egg, parsley, pepper, $1/2$ cup Romano, and $3/4$ teaspoon salt. In small bowl, with fork, mix bread crumbs and milk to form a thick paste. Add bread-crumb mixture to meat mixture; mix just until well blended but not overmixed. Shape mixture into about seventy 1-inch meatballs, handling meat as little as possible. Place meatballs on cookie sheet; cover and refrigerate 30 minutes.

3. Transfer chicken to large bowl. When cool enough to handle, remove skin and bones from chicken. Cut chicken into bite-size pieces; set aside 2 cups. (Reserve remaining chicken for another use.)

4. Strain broth chicken was cooked in through sieve lined with paper towels into large bowl; discard solids. Let stand until fat separates from meat juice, 1 to 2 minutes. Skim and discard fat from surface of broth.

5. Return broth to clean saucepot; add canned broth and remaining 2 teaspoons salt; heat to boiling over high heat. Stir in carrots and celery; heat to boiling. Reduce heat to low; cover and simmer until vegetables are tender, 8 to 10 minutes. Add meatballs and remaining $^1/_4$ cup Romano; heat to boiling over high heat. Reduce heat to low; cover and simmer until meatballs are cooked through, about 15 minutes. Stir in escarole and the 2 cups reserved chicken; heat through. Serve with additional Romano.

EACH SERVING **About 235 calories** | **18g protein** | **10g carbohydrate** | **13g total fat (5g saturated)** | **61mg cholesterol** | **760mg sodium.**

Pasta e Fagioli

A fast-lane version of our favorite Italian bean soup.

PREP 10 minutes   **COOK** 25 minutes   **MAKES** about 8 cups or 4 main-dish servings.

1 tablespoon olive oil

1 small onion, sliced

1 large stalk celery, sliced

1 can (14½ ounces) chicken broth

2 cups water

1 can (15 to 19 ounces) white kidney beans (cannellini), rinsed and drained

1 can (14½ ounces) diced tomatoes

2 garlic cloves, crushed with garlic press

1 teaspoon sugar

¼ teaspoon salt

¼ teaspoon ground black pepper

¼ cup tubettini or ditalini pasta

1 package (10 ounces) frozen chopped spinach

1. In 5- to 6-quart Dutch oven, heat oil over medium heat until hot. Add onion and celery and cook until vegetables are tender, about 10 minutes.

2. Meanwhile, in 2-quart saucepan, heat broth and water to boiling over high heat.

3. Add beans, tomatoes, garlic, sugar, salt, and pepper to Dutch oven; heat to boiling over high heat. Add broth mixture and pasta; heat to boiling. Reduce heat to medium and cook 5 minutes. Add frozen spinach; cook, stirring frequently, 3 to 4 minutes longer.

EACH SERVING About 220 calories | 10g protein | 33g carbohydrate | 5g total fat (1g saturated) | 0mg cholesterol | 1,265mg sodium.

Meat, Poultry & Fish

Grilled Chicken Breasts Saltimbocca
recipe on page 45

Tuscan Pan-Seared Strip Steak

Tuscan cooks know that a squeeze of fresh lemon juice is the perfect flavor accent for a rich cut of beef.

PREP 5 minutes **COOK** 12 minutes **MAKES** 4 main-dish servings.

4 boneless beef strip (shell) steaks, 1 inch thick (8 ounces each)

2 teaspoons olive oil

1 teaspoon dried rosemary, crumbled

1 teaspoon salt

1 teaspoon coarsely ground black pepper

4 lemon wedges

1. Heat 12-inch skillet over high heat until very hot. Brush steaks with olive oil. In small bowl, combine rosemary, salt, and pepper. Use to rub on steaks.

2. Place steaks in skillet; reduce heat to medium-high. Cook steaks 7 minutes; turn and cook 5 minutes longer for medium-rare or 7 minutes longer for medium. Serve with lemon wedges.

EACH SERVING About 375 calories | 49g protein | 1g carbohydrate | 18g total fat (6g saturated) | 129mg cholesterol | 699mg sodium.

Braciole

Serve these beef rolls with a side of pasta, topped with a sprinkling of Parmesan cheese.

PREP 30 minutes **COOK** 40 minutes **MAKES** 4 main-dish servings.

1 1/2 cups fresh bread crumbs
(about 3 slices bread)

1/3 cup freshly grated Parmesan
cheese

1/3 cup chopped fresh basil

3 tablespoons dried currants

3/4 teaspoon salt

8 thin slices beef top round
(1 pound)

1 tablespoon olive oil

3 garlic cloves, crushed with side of
chef's knife

2 cups chopped canned tomatoes
with their juice

1/3 cup chicken broth

3 strips (3" by 1/2" each) orange peel

1. In medium bowl, combine bread crumbs, Parmesan, basil, currants, and 1/4 teaspoon salt.

2. With meat mallet, or between two sheets of plastic wrap or waxed paper with rolling pin, pound beef slices to 1/8-inch thickness. Sprinkle one side of slices with remaining 1/2 teaspoon salt. Spoon bread-crumb mixture on top, pressing so it adheres to meat. From one short end, roll up each meat slice jelly-roll fashion. Secure each roll with toothpicks.

3. In nonstick 10-inch skillet, heat oil over medium heat until very hot. Add beef and cook, turning rolls, until browned, about 5 minutes. Add garlic and cook 30 seconds. Add tomatoes with their juice, broth, and orange peel; heat to boiling. Reduce heat; cover and simmer until meat is tender, about 30 minutes. Remove and discard orange peel and toothpicks before serving braciole with pan sauce.

EACH SERVING About 310 calories | 33g protein | 20g carbohydrate |
11g total fat (3g saturated) | 72mg cholesterol | 984mg sodium.

Steak Pizzaiola

Made with ingredients typically found at neighborhood pizzerias, this is perfect fare for a midweek supper. If you like, serve over grilled Italian bread.

PREP 15 minutes **COOK** 15 minutes **MAKES** 4 main-dish servings.

2 tablespoons olive oil

1 large onion (12 ounces), thinly sliced

2 garlic cloves, finely chopped

1 large red pepper, thinly sliced

1 large yellow pepper, thinly sliced

4 ounces mushrooms, trimmed and thickly sliced

1 can (15 ounces) crushed tomatoes

3/4 teaspoon salt

8 beef minute steaks (2 ounces each)

1. In nonreactive 12-inch skillet, heat 1 tablespoon oil over medium heat. Add onion and garlic and cook, stirring frequently, until onion is tender-crisp, about 2 minutes.

2. Add red and yellow peppers and mushrooms and cook, stirring frequently, until peppers are tender-crisp, about 2 minutes longer. Add tomatoes with their juice and 1/4 teaspoon salt; cook just until sauce has slightly thickened, about 2 minutes longer. Transfer to medium bowl; keep warm.

3. Wipe skillet with paper towels, then heat remaining 1 tablespoon oil over medium-high heat until very hot. Sprinkle beef with remaining 1/2 teaspoon salt; cook steaks, in batches, until just cooked through, about 2 minutes per side. Transfer steaks to warm platter as they are cooked. Spoon sauce over steaks.

EACH SERVING About 355 calories | 26g protein | 14g carbohydrate | 22g total fat (7g saturated) | 72mg cholesterol | 668mg sodium.

Stuffed Breast of Veal

This cut of meat can always be counted on for being moist, flavorful, and easy on the wallet. Here, it is filled with the classic Sicilian combination of spinach and golden raisins. Serve it hot or at room temperature; either way, it will be equally delicious.

PREP 25 minutes plus cooling **BAKE** 2 hours 15 minutes
MAKES 6 main-dish servings.

1 tablespoon olive oil	1 lemon
1 small onion, chopped	$^1/_3$ cup golden raisins
3 garlic cloves, finely chopped	$^3/_4$ teaspoon salt
2 packages (10 ounces each) frozen chopped spinach, thawed and squeezed dry	1 bone-in veal breast (4 pounds), with pocket for stuffing
	1 cup chicken broth

1. Preheat oven to 425°F. In 12-inch skillet, heat oil over medium-low heat. Add onion and garlic and cook, stirring frequently, until onion is tender, about 5 minutes. Add spinach and cook, stirring frequently, until liquid has evaporated, about 2 minutes. Remove from heat.

2. From lemon, grate $^3/_4$ teaspoon peel and squeeze 2 tablespoons juice; set juice aside. Add raisins, $^1/_2$ teaspoon salt, and lemon peel to spinach. Cool to room temperature. Spoon spinach mixture into pocket of veal.

3. Place breast, meat side up, in medium roasting pan (14" by 10"). Sprinkle remaining $^1/_4$ teaspoon salt on meat side (not rib side) of veal and roast 1 hour. Turn veal, rib side up, and pour broth and lemon juice into bottom of roasting pan. Cover veal with loose tent of foil and bake until tender, about 1 hour and 15 minutes longer.

4. Transfer veal to cutting board, rib side down, and let stand 10 minutes to set juices for easier carving. Skim and discard fat from drippings in pan. Carve veal by slicing down along one rib bone. Cut away rib bone and discard, then continue carving. Transfer slices to warm platter and serve with pan juices.

EACH SERVING About 425 calories | 51g protein | 13g carbohydrate | 18g total fat (6g saturated) | 183mg cholesterol | 637mg sodium.

Vitello Tonnato

Serve this delicious cold buffet dish with bowls of roasted red peppers, green beans, a variety of olives, and lots of crusty bread.

PREP 20 minutes plus cooling and chilling   **COOK** 1 hour 50 minutes
MAKES 8 main-dish servings.

1 rolled boneless veal shoulder roast ($2^3/4$ to 3 pounds), trimmed and tied

10 anchovy fillets

2 garlic cloves, thinly sliced

3 cups water

1 can ($14^1/2$ ounces) chicken broth

1 cup dry white wine

1 medium onion, thinly sliced

2 carrots, peeled and thinly sliced

1 can (6 ounces) tuna packed in oil, undrained

$^1/2$ cup mayonnaise

$^1/2$ cup heavy or whipping cream

1 tablespoon fresh lemon juice

$^1/2$ teaspoon salt

$^1/4$ teaspoon dried sage

2 tablespoons chopped fresh parsley

1. With sharp knife, make slits all over veal. Coarsely chop 2 anchovies; insert chopped anchovies and garlic into slits.

2. In nonreactive 5-quart Dutch oven, combine water, broth, wine, onion, and carrots and heat to boiling over medium heat. Add roast to Dutch oven. Reduce heat; cover and simmer until veal is tender, about 1 hour and 45 minutes.

3. Remove from heat; let veal cool in broth 1 hour, then transfer veal to plate and refrigerate to cool completely. Strain broth, reserving $^3/4$ cup; discard remaining broth. Transfer reserved broth to food processor fitted with knife blade. Add tuna, mayonnaise, cream, lemon juice, salt, sage, and remaining 8 anchovies; puree.

4. Cut veal into thin slices and transfer to deep platter or shallow casserole large enough to hold veal in one or two layers. Pour sauce over veal; cover and refrigerate at least 1 hour or up to 24 hours. Serve chilled or at room temperature, sprinkled with parsley.

EACH SERVING About 401 calories | 37g protein | 3g carbohydrate | 26g total fat (7g saturated) | 172mg cholesterol | 801mg sodium.

Osso Buco with Gremolata

This aromatic recipe from **Northern Italy** is especially wonderful when served with Risotto Milanese (page 74) or Creamy Polenta (page 75).

PREP 40 minutes   **BAKE** 2 hours   **MAKES** 4 main-dish servings.

4 meaty veal shank cross cuts (osso buco), each about 2 inches thick (1 pound each)

1/2 teaspoon salt

1/4 teaspoon ground black pepper

1 tablespoon olive oil

2 medium onions, chopped

3 carrots, peeled and chopped

2 stalks celery, chopped

4 garlic cloves, finely chopped

1 can (14 to 16 ounces) tomatoes in puree

1 cup dry white wine

1 cup chicken broth

1 bay leaf

2 tablespoons chopped fresh parsley

1/2 teaspoon freshly grated lemon peel

1. Preheat oven to 350°F. Sprinkle shanks with salt and pepper. In nonreactive 5-quart Dutch oven, heat oil over medium-high heat until very hot. Add shanks and cook until browned, about 10 minutes, transferring shanks to plate as they are browned. Add onions to Dutch oven and cook over medium heat, stirring occasionally, until slightly browned, about 5 minutes. Add carrots, celery, and three-fourths of garlic; cook 2 minutes longer.

2. Return veal to Dutch oven. Stir in tomatoes with their puree, wine, broth, and bay leaf. Heat to boiling over high heat. Cover and place in oven. Bake until veal is tender when pierced with fork, about 2 hours.

3. Meanwhile, prepare gremolata: In small bowl, mix parsley, lemon peel, and remaining garlic. Cover and refrigerate until ready to serve.

4. Transfer veal to platter. Heat sauce in Dutch oven to boiling over high heat; boil until it has reduced to 4 cups, about 10 minutes. Discard bay leaf. Pour sauce over veal and sprinkle with gremolata.

EACH SERVING About 374 calories | 53g protein | 20g carbohydrate | 8g total fat (2g saturated) | 183mg cholesterol | 874mg sodium.

Veal with Tomato and Arugula Salad

Perfect for summer: Crispy veal cutlets topped with a zesty salad of contrasting color, flavor, and texture.

PREP 20 minutes   **COOK** 10 minutes   **MAKES** 4 main-dish servings.

2 teaspoons fresh lemon juice

6 tablespoons olive oil

1 teaspoon salt

³/₄ teaspoon ground black pepper

1 large tomato (12 ounces), coarsely chopped

1 cup loosely packed basil leaves

¹/₄ cup coarsely chopped red onion

1 pound veal cutlets

2 large eggs

¹/₂ cup all-purpose flour

1 cup plain dried bread crumbs

1 bunch arugula (10 ounces), trimmed

1. In medium bowl, combine lemon juice, 2 tablespoons oil, ¹/₂ teaspoon salt, and ¹/₄ teaspoon pepper. Stir in tomato, basil, and onion; set aside.

2. With meat mallet, or between two sheets of plastic wrap or waxed paper with rolling pin, pound cutlets to ¹/₈-inch thickness. In pie plate, beat eggs with remaining ¹/₂ teaspoon each salt and pepper. Place flour on waxed paper; place bread crumbs on separate waxed paper. Dip cutlets in flour, then in egg mixture, then in bread crumbs.

3. In nonstick 12-inch skillet, heat 2 tablespoons oil over medium-high heat until very hot. Add half of cutlets and cook about 3 minutes per side. Transfer to platter large enough to hold cutlets in single layer; keep warm. Repeat with remaining 2 tablespoons oil and remaining veal.

4. Add arugula to tomato mixture and toss to combine. Spoon on top of hot veal.

EACH SERVING About 538 calories | 35g protein | 39g carbohydrate | 27g total fat (5g saturated) | 195mg cholesterol | 939mg sodium.

Veal Scallopini Marsala

This sensational dish takes only minutes to prepare.

PREP 10 minutes **COOK** 15 minutes **MAKES** 6 main-dish servings.

1 pound veal cutlets	3 tablespoons butter or margarine
$^{1}/_{4}$ cup all-purpose flour	$^{1}/_{2}$ cup dry Marsala wine
$^{1}/_{4}$ teaspoon salt	$^{1}/_{2}$ cup chicken broth
$^{1}/_{8}$ teaspoon coarsely ground pepper	1 tablespoon chopped fresh parsley

1. With meat mallet, or between two sheets of plastic wrap or waxed paper with rolling pin, pound cutlets to $^{1}/_{8}$-inch thickness. Cut cutlets into 3" by 3" pieces. On waxed paper, combine flour, salt, and pepper; coat veal with seasoned flour, shaking off excess.

2. In nonstick 10-inch skillet, melt butter over medium-high heat. Cook veal, in batches, until lightly browned, 45 to 60 seconds per side, using slotted spatula to transfer pieces to warm platter as they are browned; keep warm.

3. Stir Marsala and broth into veal drippings in pan; cook until syrupy, 4 to 5 minutes, stirring until browned bits are loosened from bottom of skillet. Pour sauce over veal and sprinkle with parsley.

EACH SERVING About 179 calories | 17g protein | 5g carbohydrate | 7g total fat (4g saturated) | 75mg cholesterol | 288mg sodium.

Sicilian Stuffed Pork Chops

Golden raisins give the stuffing a slightly sweet note. If you can't find chard, spinach works equally well.

PREP 20 minutes   **COOK** 1 hour 10 minutes   **MAKES** 4 main-dish servings.

12 ounces Swiss chard, tough stems trimmed and leaves thinly sliced (4 cups)

4 teaspoons olive oil

1 garlic clove, minced

1/4 cup golden raisins

2 tablespoons pine nuts (pignoli), toasted and chopped

3/4 teaspoon salt

4 pork loin chops, 1 1/2 inches thick (10 ounces each)

1/4 teaspoon ground black pepper

1 cup chicken broth

1/3 cup dry white wine

1. In 2-quart saucepan, heat Swiss chard and *1 inch water* to boiling over high heat; cover and cook 5 minutes. Transfer chard to sieve; rinse with cold water until cool. With back of spoon, press to remove excess liquid.

2. In same saucepan, heat 1 teaspoon oil over medium heat. Add garlic and cook 30 seconds. Remove pan from heat; stir in chard, raisins, pine nuts, and 1/4 teaspoon salt until well combined.

3. Pat pork dry with paper towels. Holding knife parallel to surface, cut horizontal pocket in each chop. Fill pockets with chard mixture. Gently press pockets closed to seal in stuffing; secure with toothpicks. Sprinkle chops with remaining 1/2 teaspoon salt and pepper.

4. In nonstick 12-inch skillet, heat remaining 3 teaspoons oil over medium-high heat until very hot. Add chops and cook until well browned, about 4 minutes per side. Add broth and wine to skillet; heat to boiling. Reduce heat; cover and simmer until chops are tender, about 1 hour.

5. Transfer chops to platter; keep warm. Increase heat to high and heat pan juices to boiling; boil until juices have been reduced to 3/4 cup. Skim and discard fat from juices and serve with chops.

EACH SERVING About 400 calories | 46g protein | 12g carbohydrate | 19g total fat (5g saturated) | 117mg cholesterol | 973mg sodium.

Italian Sausage and Broccoli Rabe

In this rustic classic, sweet sausage balances the appealing bitterness of broccoli rabe. Fans of this green may want to double the amount used.

PREP 5 minutes **COOK** 30 minutes **MAKES** 4 main-dish servings.

1 bunch broccoli rabe (1 pound), tough ends trimmed

2 teaspoons salt

1 pound sweet Italian-sausage links, pricked with fork

¹/₄ cup water

1 tablespoon olive oil

1 large garlic clove, finely chopped

¹/₈ teaspoon crushed red pepper

1. In 5-quart saucepot, heat *4 quarts water* to boiling. Add broccoli rabe and salt. Cook just until stems are tender, about 5 minutes; drain. When cool enough to handle, coarsely chop broccoli rabe.

2. Meanwhile, in 10-inch skillet, heat sausage links and water to boiling over medium heat. Cover and cook 5 minutes. Remove cover and cook, turning sausages frequently, until water has evaporated and sausages are well browned, about 20 minutes longer. With tongs, transfer sausages to paper towels to drain; cut each sausage on diagonal in half.

3. Discard fat from skillet but do not wipe clean. To drippings in skillet, add oil, garlic, and crushed red pepper. Cook, stirring, until fragrant, about 15 seconds. Add broccoli rabe and cook, stirring, until well coated and heated through, about 2 minutes. Stir in sausages and remove from heat.

EACH SERVING About 325 calories | 19g protein | 6g carbohydrate | 25g total fat (8g saturated) | 65mg cholesterol 1,079mg sodium.

Italian Sausage and Peppers

For this old-fashioned favorite, use sweet or hot sausage, green or red peppers, or a combination.

PREP 10 minutes **COOK** 30 minutes **MAKES** 6 main-dish servings.

1 1/2 pounds hot or sweet Italian-sausage links, pricked with fork

1/4 cup water

2 large green or red peppers, cut into 3/4-inch-wide strips

2 large onions (12 ounces each), cut into 1/2-inch-thick slices

1 garlic clove, finely chopped

1/4 teaspoon salt

1. In 12-inch skillet, heat sausage links and water to boiling over medium heat. Cover and cook 5 minutes. Remove cover and cook, turning sausages frequently, until water has evaporated and sausages are well browned, about 20 minutes longer. With tongs, transfer sausages to paper towels to drain.

2. Pour off all but 1 tablespoon fat from skillet. Add peppers, onions, garlic, and salt; cook over medium heat, stirring frequently, until vegetables are tender.

3. Add cooked sausage links to peppers and onions; heat through.

EACH SERVING About 322 calories | 18g protein | 10g carbohydrate | 23g total fat (8g saturated) | 66mg cholesterol | 874mg sodium.

Roast Chicken with Basil Gremolata

Gremolata, a flavorful Italian garnish, is usually made with garlic, lemon peel, and parsley; using basil adds a hint of sweetness.

PREP 15 minutes **ROAST** 1 hour **MAKES** 4 main-dish servings.

1 chicken (about 3 1/2 pounds)	1/2 teaspoon salt
10 large basil leaves	1/4 teaspoon coarsely ground black pepper
1 whole head garlic	
1 lemon, cut crosswise into thin slices	1/2 teaspoon finely grated lemon peel

1. Preheat oven to 450°F. Remove giblets and neck from chicken; reserve for another use. Rinse chicken inside and out with cold running water; drain well. Pat dry with paper towels.

2. With fingertips, gently separate skin from meat on chicken breast. Place 2 basil leaves under the skin of each breast half. Remove 1 garlic clove from head of garlic; reserve for making gremolata. Cut head of garlic horizontally in half; place inside cavity of chicken with lemon slices. Sprinkle salt and pepper on outside of chicken.

3. With chicken breast side up, lift wings up toward neck, then fold wing tips under back of chicken so wings stay in place. Tie legs together with kitchen string. Place chicken, breast side up, on rack in medium roasting pan (14" by 10").

4. Roast chicken about 1 hour. Chicken is done when temperature on meat thermometer inserted in thickest part of the thigh, next to body, reaches 175° to 180°F, and juices run clear when thigh is pierced with tip of knife.

5. Meanwhile, prepare gremolata: Mince together grated lemon peel, reserved garlic clove, and remaining 6 basil leaves.

6. Transfer chicken to warm platter; let stand 10 minutes to set juices for easier carving. Remove skin from chicken before eating, if desired. Sprinkle with gremolata.

EACH SERVING WITHOUT SKIN About 275 calories | 42g protein | 0g carbohydrate | 11g total fat (3g saturated) | 129mg cholesterol | 390mg sodium.

Chicken Cacciatore

Dishes prepared *alla cacciatore*, "hunter-style," include mushrooms in the sauce. This is the kind of home cooking that found its way first into Italian restaurants in the U.S. and then into American kitchens. Serve over wide, flat noodles.

PREP 15 minutes   **COOK** 40 minutes   **MAKES** 4 main-dish servings.

2 tablespoons olive oil

1 chicken (3¹/₂ pounds), cut into 8 pieces and skin removed from all but wings

3 tablespoons all-purpose flour

1 medium onion, finely chopped

4 garlic cloves, crushed with garlic press

8 ounces mushrooms, trimmed and thickly sliced

1 can (14 to 16 ounces) tomatoes

¹/₂ teaspoon salt

¹/₂ teaspoon dried oregano, crumbled

¹/₄ teaspoon dried sage

¹/₈ teaspoon ground red pepper (cayenne)

1. In nonstick 12-inch skillet, heat oil over medium-high heat until very hot. On waxed paper, coat chicken with flour, shaking off excess. Add chicken to skillet and cook until golden brown, about 3 minutes per side. With slotted spoon, transfer chicken pieces to bowl as they are browned.

2. Add onion and garlic to skillet. Reduce heat to medium-low and cook, stirring occasionally, until onion is tender, about 5 minutes. Add mushrooms and cook, stirring frequently, until just tender, about 3 minutes.

3. Add tomatoes with their juice, breaking them up with spoon. Add salt, oregano, sage, ground red pepper, and chicken, and heat to boiling over high heat. Reduce heat; cover and simmer until juices run clear when thickest part of chicken is pierced with tip of knife, about 25 minutes.

4. Transfer chicken to serving bowl. Spoon sauce over chicken.

EACH SERVING About 371 calories | 44g protein | 18g carbohydrate | 13g total fat (3g saturated) | 133mg cholesterol | 608mg sodium.

Grilled Chicken Breasts Saltimbocca

In Italian, *saltimbocca* means "jump in your mouth," and these irresistible prosciutto and sage–topped chicken breasts will do just that. Try it with turkey cutlets, too. (See photo on page 27.)

PREP 5 minutes **GRILL** 10 minutes **MAKES** 4 main-dish servings.

4 medium skinless, boneless chicken breast halves (1¹/₂ pounds)

¹/₈ teaspoon salt

¹/₈ teaspoon ground black pepper

12 fresh sage leaves

4 large slices prosciutto (4 ounces)

1. Prepare grill. Sprinkle chicken with salt and pepper. Place 3 sage leaves on each breast half. Place 1 prosciutto slice on top of each breast half, tucking in edges if necessary; secure with toothpicks.

2. Arrange chicken, prosciutto side down, on grill rack over medium heat and grill 5 to 6 minutes. Turn and grill until chicken loses its pink color throughout, 5 to 6 minutes longer.

EACH SERVING About 223 calories | 41g protein | 0g carbohydrate | 6g total fat (1g saturated) | 105mg cholesterol | 690mg sodium.

Chicken Parmesan

This grilled version of an old favorite still has a melted layer of mozzarella and a sprinkling of grated Parmesan, but we've replaced the usual tomato sauce with juicy slices of tomato and fresh basil leaves.

PREP 10 minutes   **GRILL** 10 minutes   **MAKES** 4 main-dish servings

4 medium skinless, boneless chicken-breast halves (1$^{1}/_{4}$ pounds)

2 teaspoons olive oil

$^{1}/_{2}$ teaspoon salt

$^{1}/_{4}$ teaspoon coarsely ground black pepper

4 ounces part-skim mozzarella cheese, cut into $^{1}/_{4}$-inch-thick slices and each slice cut crosswise in half

2 medium tomatoes, cut into $^{1}/_{4}$-inch-thick slices

$^{1}/_{4}$ cup freshly grated Parmesan cheese

$^{3}/_{4}$ cup loosely packed fresh basil leaves

1. Prepare grill. If necessary, pound cutlets to uniform $^{1}/_{4}$-inch thickness. Coat chicken with oil and sprinkle with salt and pepper.

2. Arrange chicken on grill rack over medium-high heat and grill 4 minutes. Turn chicken and top with mozzarella, tomatoes, and Parmesan. Grill until chicken loses its pink color throughout, 4 to 6 minutes longer.

3. Transfer chicken to warm platter and top with basil leaves.

EACH SERVING About 340 calories | 49g protein | 4g carbohydrate | 13g total fat (5g saturated) | 129mg cholesterol | 615mg sodium.

Sicilian Tuna

A robust sauce of tomatoes, Kalamata olives, capers, and chopped fresh basil complements the flavor of the marinated tuna steaks.

PREP 25 minutes plus marinating **BROIL** 6 minutes **MAKES** 8 main-dish servings.

6 tablespoons olive oil

5 tablespoons fresh lemon juice

4 anchovy fillets, chopped

I garlic clove, finely chopped

$^{1}/_{4}$ teaspoon dried thyme

$^{1}/_{8}$ teaspoon ground black pepper

8 tuna steaks, $^{3}/_{4}$ inch thick
(5 ounces each)

I large stalk celery, chopped

3 ripe medium plum tomatoes, chopped

2 green onions, sliced

$^{1}/_{4}$ cup pitted Kalamata or Niçoise olives, coarsely chopped

2 tablespoons capers, drained

$^{1}/_{4}$ cup chopped fresh basil

1. In 13" by 9" baking dish, combine 3 tablespoons oil, 3 tablespoons lemon juice, anchovies, garlic, thyme, and pepper. Add tuna, turning to coat. Cover and refrigerate fish at least 45 minutes or up to 2 hours to marinate, turning once.

2. In 2-quart saucepan, heat remaining 3 tablespoons oil over medium heat. Add celery and cook 5 minutes. Stir in tomatoes, green onions, olives, and capers; cook until mixture has thickened slightly, about 5 minutes. Stir in basil and remaining 2 tablespoons lemon juice; keep warm.

3. Preheat broiler. Place tuna on rack in broiling pan. Place pan in broiler at closest position to heat source. Broil tuna until pale pink in center (medium), about 3 minutes per side or until desired doneness. Serve tuna with sauce.

EACH SERVING About 239 calories | 24g protein | 3g carbohydrate | 14g total fat (2g saturated) | 39mg cholesterol | 291mg sodium.

Grilled Tuna with Tuscan White Beans

Serve tuna slices on a bed of warm cannellini beans seasoned with lemon, garlic, and sage.

PREP 35 minutes **GRILL** 3 minutes **MAKES** 4 main-dish servings.

1 lemon

1 tablespoon plus 3 teaspoons extravirgin olive oil

1 medium onion, chopped

1 medium stalk celery, finely chopped

2 garlic cloves, crushed with garlic press

1 tablespoon fresh sage leaves (about 6 large), thinly sliced

2 cans (15 to 19 ounces each) white kidney beans (cannellini), rinsed and drained

1 teaspoon salt

$^1/_2$ teaspoon coarsely ground black pepper

1 pound tuna steak, 1 inch thick, cut into $^1/_2$-inch-thick slices

2 medium plum tomatoes, finely chopped

1 tablespoon chopped fresh parsley leaves

1. Grate $^1/_2$ teaspoon peel and squeeze 2 tablespoons juice from lemon.

2. In 3-quart saucepan, heat 1 tablespoon plus 1 teaspoon oil over medium heat. Add onion and celery, and cook, stirring occasionally, until tender, about 12 minutes. Add garlic, sage, and lemon peel and cook, stirring, 1 minute. Add beans, lemon juice, $^1/_2$ teaspoon salt, and $^1/_4$ teaspoon pepper and cook, stirring gently, until heated through, about 2 minutes.

3. Meanwhile, brush both sides of tuna with remaining 2 teaspoons oil and sprinkle with remaining $^1/_2$ teaspoon salt and $^1/_4$ teaspoon pepper.

4. Heat grill pan over medium-high heat until hot. Add tuna and cook, turning once, until it just loses its pink color throughout, 3 to 4 minutes. (Or, preheat broiler. Place tuna on rack in broiling pan. Place pan in broiler at closest position to heat source. Broil tuna 3 to 4 minutes.)

5. Spoon warm bean mixture onto platter and top with tuna. Sprinkle with chopped tomatoes and parsley.

EACH SERVING About 412 calories | 41g protein | 45g carbohydrate | 9g total fat (2g saturated) | 50mg cholesterol | 1118mg sodium.

Snapper Livornese

Vibrant with olives, capers, and basil, this preparation works beautifully with any lean white fish.

PREP 10 minutes **COOK** 25 minutes **MAKES** 4 main-dish servings.

1 tablespoon olive oil

1 garlic clove, finely chopped

1 can (14 to 16 ounces) tomatoes

$^1/_8$ teaspoon salt

$^1/_8$ teaspoon ground black pepper

4 red snapper fillets (6 ounces each)

$^1/_4$ cup chopped fresh basil

$^1/_4$ cup Kalamata or Gaeta olives, pitted and chopped

2 teaspoons capers, drained

1. In nonstick 10-inch skillet, heat oil over medium heat. Add garlic and cook just until very fragrant, about 30 seconds. Stir in tomatoes with their juice, salt, and pepper, breaking up tomatoes with side of spoon. Heat to boiling; reduce heat and simmer 10 minutes.

2. With tweezers, remove any bones from snapper fillets. Place fillets, skin side down, in skillet. Cover and simmer until fish is just opaque through-out, about 10 minutes. With wide slotted spatula, transfer fish to warm platter. Stir basil, olives, and capers into tomato sauce and spoon over snapper.

EACH SERVING About 250 calories | 36g protein | 6g carbohydrate | 8g total fat (1g saturated) | 63mg cholesterol | 571mg sodium.

Fried Calamari Fra Diavolo

Crispy golden-fried squid is served with a tomato dipping sauce that is often as spicy as the devil (*fra diavolo* means "in the style of" or "mixed up" with the devil). The calamari are also delicious with a squeeze of lemon.

PREP 10 minutes   **COOK** 25 minutes   **MAKES** 4 first-course servings.

I tablespoon olive oil

2 garlic cloves, crushed with side of chef's knife

$^1/_8$ to $^1/_4$ teaspoon crushed red pepper

I can (14 to 16 ounces) tomatoes

$^3/_4$ teaspoon salt

I pound cleaned squid

$^2/_3$ cup all-purpose flour

I cup water

vegetable oil for frying

1. In nonreactive 1-quart saucepan, heat olive oil over medium heat. Add garlic and crushed red pepper; cook until garlic is golden, about 30 seconds. Add tomatoes with their juice and $^1/_2$ teaspoon salt, breaking up tomatoes with side of spoon; heat to boiling. Reduce heat; cover and simmer 10 minutes. Keep warm.

2. Rinse squid with cold running water and gently pat dry with paper towels. Slice squid bodies crosswise into $^3/_4$-inch rings. Cut tentacles into pieces if large.

3. In small bowl, with fork, mix flour and water until smooth. In 10-inch skillet, heat $^1/_2$ inch vegetable oil over medium heat until very hot. (A small piece of bread dropped into oil should sink, then rise to top and begin bubbling.) In small batches, drop squid into batter, allowing excess to drip off. Add squid to hot oil and fry, turning once or twice, until coating is golden, about 2 minutes. With slotted spoon, transfer squid to paper towels to drain. Sprinkle with remaining $^1/_4$ teaspoon salt. Serve with tomato sauce for dipping.

EACH SERVING About 325 calories | 21g protein | 25g carbohydrate | 16g total fat (2g saturated) | 264mg cholesterol | 660mg sodium.

Pasta, Grains & Beans

Penne Arrabbiata
recipe on page 54

Bucatini all'Amatriciana

Named for the town of Amatrice, near Rome, this sauce gets its distinctive character from pancetta and dried red chiles called *diavoletti,* "little devils." We've substituted crushed red pepper.

PREP 10 minutes   **COOK** 45 minutes   **MAKES** 4 main-dish servings.

1 tablespoon olive oil	$^1/_2$ teaspoon salt
4 ounces sliced pancetta, chopped	1 package (16 ounces) bucatini or rigatoni
1 small onion, chopped	
1 garlic clove, finely chopped	$^1/_4$ cup chopped fresh parsley
$^1/_4$ teaspoon crushed red pepper	$^1/_4$ cup freshly grated Pecorino Romano cheese
1 can (28 ounces) plum tomatoes	

1. In nonreactive 5-quart Dutch oven, heat oil over medium heat. Add pancetta and cook, stirring, until lightly browned, about 5 minutes. Stir in onion and cook until tender, about 3 minutes. Stir in garlic and crushed red pepper; cook 15 seconds. Add tomatoes with their juice and salt; heat to boiling, breaking up tomatoes with side of spoon. Reduce heat and simmer, stirring occasionally, 30 minutes.

2. Meanwhile, in large saucepot, cook pasta as label directs. Drain. In warm serving bowl, toss pasta with sauce and parsley. Serve with freshly grated Pecorino Romano cheese.

EACH SERVING About 654 calories | 23g protein | 97g carbohydrate | 20g total fat (8g saturated) | 21mg cholesterol | 993mg sodium.

Penne Arrabbiata

In nonreactive 5-quart Dutch oven, **cook 4 slices bacon,** cut into $^1/_2$-inch pieces, over medium heat, stirring occasionally, until browned. With slotted spoon, transfer bacon to paper towels to drain. Discard all but 1 tablespoon bacon drippings. Drain **1 can (28 ounces) plum tomatoes,** reserving $^1/_2$ cup juice. Coarsely chop tomatoes. Add **1 garlic clove,** crushed with garlic press, to Dutch oven and cook over medium heat, stirring, 30 seconds. Add tomatoes, reserved tomato juice, **2 tablespoons chopped fresh parsley leaves**, **¹/₄ teaspoon salt**, and **¹/₈ to ¹/₄ teaspoon crushed red pepper** and cook, stirring occasionally, 10 minutes. Meanwhile, in large saucepot, cook **1 package (16 ounces) penne pasta** as label directs. Drain pasta. In warm large serving bowl, toss pasta with sauce, **¹/₄ cup freshly grated Pecorino Romano cheese**, and bacon; garnish with **parsley leaves**. Serve with additional Romano, if you like. Makes 4 main-dish servings.

EACH SERVING About 540 calories | 20g protein | 93g carbohydrate | 10g total fat (4g saturated) | 14mg cholesterol | 705mg sodium.

Orecchiette alla Vodka

A restaurant favorite that's fast to fix at home. We use orecchiette (literally, "little ears") for our version, but it also works well with other short pastas like penne or rotini.

PREP 15 minutes COOK about 15 minutes MAKES 4 main-dish servings

1 package (16 ounces) orecchiette or
   bow-tie pasta

1 can (14 to 16 ounces) tomatoes in
   juice, drained

1/2 cup heavy or whipping cream

1/2 cup milk

3 tablespoons vodka (optional)

4 teaspoons tomato paste

1/2 teaspoon salt

1/8 to 1/4 teaspoon crushed
   red pepper

1 cup frozen peas, thawed

1/2 cup loosely packed fresh basil
   leaves, thinly sliced

1. In large saucepot, cook pasta as label directs.

2. Meanwhile, chop tomatoes. In nonreactive 2-quart saucepan, heat tomatoes, cream, milk, vodka, if using, tomato paste, salt, and crushed red pepper over medium-low heat just to simmering. Stir in peas and heat through.

3. Drain pasta; return to saucepot. Add tomato cream sauce; toss well. Sprinkle with basil.

EACH SERVING About 590 calories | 19g protein | 98g carbohydrate | 15g total fat (8g saturated) | 45mg cholesterol | 635mg sodium.

Farfalle with Gorgonzola Sauce

Farfalle, which means "butterflies" in Italian, are commonly called bow ties. We've combined them with a creamy blue-cheese sauce and a sprinkling of toasted walnuts.

PREP 10 minutes   **COOK** 25 minutes   **MAKES** 6 main-dish servings.

1 package (16 ounces) bow ties or penne

1 cup half-and-half or light cream

$^3/_4$ cup chicken broth

4 ounces Gorgonzola or other blue cheese, crumbled

$^1/_4$ teaspoon coarsely ground black pepper

1 cup frozen peas, thawed

$^1/_2$ cup chopped walnuts, toasted

1. In large saucepot, cook pasta as label directs. Drain.

2. Meanwhile, in 2-quart saucepan, heat half-and-half and broth just to boiling over medium-high heat. Reduce heat to medium; cook 5 minutes. Add Gorgonzola and pepper and cook, stirring constantly, until cheese has melted and sauce is smooth. Stir in peas.

3. In warm serving bowl, toss pasta with sauce; sprinkle with walnuts.

EACH SERVING About 486 calories | 18g protein | 63g carbohydrate | 18g total fat (8g saturated) | 31mg cholesterol | 499mg sodium.

Fettuccine Alfredo

Roman restaurateur **Alfred di Lello** created this luscious, creamy dish in the early 1900s, and its popularity has never waned. Be sure to use only freshly grated Parmesan cheese (preferably Italian Parmigiano-Reggiano) when making this indulgent pasta.

PREP 10 minutes   **COOK** 25 minutes   **MAKES** 6 accompaniment servings.

1 package (16 ounces) fettuccine

1 1/2 cups heavy or whipping cream

1 tablespoon butter or margarine

1/2 teaspoon salt

1/4 teaspoon coarsely ground black pepper

3/4 cup freshly grated Parmesan cheese

chopped fresh parsley

1. In large saucepot, cook pasta as label directs. Drain.

2. Meanwhile, in 2-quart saucepan, heat cream, butter, salt, and pepper to boiling over medium-high heat. Boil until sauce has thickened slightly, 2 to 3 minutes. In warm serving bowl, toss pasta with sauce and Parmesan. Sprinkle with parsley.

EACH SERVING About 558 calories | 16g protein | 59g carbohydrate | 29g total fat (17g saturated) | 96mg cholesterol | 532mg sodium.

Triple-Mushroom Fettuccine

The rich, earthy flavors of shiitake, cremini, and oyster mushrooms are combined with hearty fettuccine noodles to make a satisfying and easy family dish that's special enough for friends.

PREP 20 minutes **COOK** 25 minutes **MAKES** 4 main-dish servings.

- 1 package (16 ounces) fettuccine or linguine
- 2 tablespoons margarine or butter
- 1 medium onion, finely chopped
- 3 packages (4 ounces each) sliced wild mushroom blend or 1 pound mixed wild mushrooms, tough stems discarded and caps thinly sliced
- 2 garlic cloves, crushed with garlic press
- $^1/_4$ teaspoon dried thyme
- $^1/_2$ teaspoon salt
- $^1/_4$ teaspoon coarsely ground black pepper
- 1 can (14$^1/_2$ ounces) reduced-sodium chicken broth or vegetable broth
- 1 cup loosely packed fresh parsley leaves, chopped

1. In large saucepot, cook pasta as label directs.

2. Meanwhile, in nonstick 12-inch skillet, melt margarine over medium heat. Add onion and cook, stirring occasionally, until tender, 8 to 10 minutes. Increase heat to medium-high. Add mushrooms, garlic, thyme, salt, and pepper and cook, stirring often, until mushrooms are golden and liquid has evaporated, 10 minutes.

3. Add broth to mushrooms and heat to boiling, stirring occasionally.

4. Drain pasta; return to saucepot. Add mushroom mixture and parsley and toss well to coat.

EACH SERVING About 530 calories | 19g protein | 95g carbohydrate | 8g total fat (1g saturated) | 0mg cholesterol | 780mg sodium.

Spaghetti with Pesto

Pesto is the perfect way to make good use of all that fresh summer basil. If you don't plan to serve the pesto with pasta, omit the water in Step 2. To store pesto, spoon into half-pint containers and top with a few tablespoons of olive oil. Cover and refrigerate up to one week.

PREP 10 minutes **COOK** 25 minutes
MAKES 4 main-dish servings (about 3/4 cup sauce).

1 package (16 ounces) spaghetti or linguine

2 cups firmly packed fresh basil leaves

1 garlic clove, crushed with garlic press

2 tablespoons pine nuts (pignoli) or walnuts

$^1/_4$ cup olive oil

1 teaspoon salt

$^1/_4$ teaspoon coarsely ground black pepper

$^1/_2$ cup freshly grated Parmesan cheese

1. In large saucepot, cook pasta as label directs. Drain, reserving $^1/_4$ cup pasta water. Return pasta to pot; keep warm.

2. Meanwhile, in blender or in food processor with knife blade attached, puree basil, garlic, pine nuts, oil, reserved pasta water, salt, and pepper until smooth. Add Parmesan and blend until combined. Add pesto to pasta in saucepot; toss to combine.

EACH SERVING About 655 calories | 24g protein | 92g carbohydrate | 22g total fat (5g saturated) | 10mg cholesterol | 920mg sodium.

Pasta Puttanesca with Arugula

Snap up some homegrown tomatoes and showcase them in this no-cook sauce with just-right Mediterranean accents.

PREP 15 minutes   **COOK** 15 minutes   **MAKES** 4 main-dish servings.

- 1 package (16 ounces) gemelli or corkscrew pasta
- 1 1/2 pounds tomatoes (about 5 medium), cut into 1/2-inch chunks
- 1 medium shallot, minced (about 1/4 cup)
- 1 garlic clove, crushed with garlic press
- 2 tablespoons olive oil
- 2 tablespoons capers, drained and chopped
- 1 tablespoon red wine vinegar
- 1/2 teaspoon freshly grated lemon peel
- 1/4 teaspoon crushed red pepper
- 2 bunches arugula (about 4 ounces each), tough stems removed and leaves coarsely chopped
- 1 cup packed fresh basil leaves, chopped

1. In large saucepot, cook pasta as label directs.

2. Meanwhile, in large serving bowl, toss tomatoes, shallot, garlic, oil, capers, vinegar, lemon peel, and crushed red pepper until well mixed.

3. Drain pasta. Add pasta to tomato mixture and toss well. Just before serving, add arugula and basil and toss gently until greens are slightly wilted.

EACH SERVING About 540 calories | 18g protein | 97g carbohydrate | 10g total fat (1g saturated) | 0mg cholesterol | 310mg sodium.

Seafood Fra Diavolo

This classic sauce pairs a spicy tomato sauce with favorites from the sea. Depending on what's in your market, feel free to substitute local crab, clams, or scallops.

PREP 25 minutes   **COOK** I hour   **MAKES** 6 main-dish servings.

8 ounces cleaned squid

I tablespoon olive oil

I large garlic clove, finely chopped

$1/4$ teaspoon crushed red pepper

I can (28 ounces) plum tomatoes

$1/2$ teaspoon salt

I dozen mussels, scrubbed and debearded

8 ounces medium shrimp, shelled and deveined

I package (16 ounces) linguine or spaghetti

$1/4$ cup chopped fresh parsley

1. Rinse squid and pat dry with paper towels. Slice squid bodies crosswise into $1/4$-inch rings. Cut tentacles into several pieces if they are large.

2. In nonreactive 4-quart saucepan, heat oil over medium heat. Add garlic and crushed red pepper; cook just until fragrant, about 30 seconds. Stir in tomatoes with their juice and salt, breaking up tomatoes with side of spoon. Heat to boiling over high heat. Add squid and heat to boiling. Reduce heat; cover and simmer 30 minutes. Remove cover and simmer 15 minutes longer. Increase heat to high. Add mussels; cover and cook 3 minutes. Stir in shrimp; cover and cook until mussels open and shrimp are opaque throughout, about 2 minutes longer. Discard any mussels that have not opened.

3. Meanwhile, in large saucepot, cook pasta as label directs. Drain. In warm serving bowl, toss pasta with seafood mixture and parsley.

EACH SERVING About 410 calories | 25g protein | 65g carbohydrate | 5g total fat (1g saturated) | 140mg cholesterol | 588mg sodium.

Linguine with White Clam Sauce

Start with fresh clams and add a few ingredients to cook up one of the best of all pasta dishes. Don't overcook the clams, or they will become tough.

PREP 15 minutes   **COOK** 30 minutes   **MAKES** 6 main-dish servings.

$^1/_2$ **cup dry white wine**

2 dozen littleneck clams, scrubbed

1 package (16 ounces) linguine or spaghetti

$^1/_4$ **cup olive oil**

1 large garlic clove, finely chopped

$^1/_4$ **teaspoon crushed red pepper**

$^1/_4$ **cup chopped fresh parsley**

1. In nonreactive 5-quart Dutch oven, heat wine to boiling over high heat. Add clams; cook until clams open, 5 to 10 minutes, transferring clams to bowl as they open. Discard any clams that have not opened.

2. Strain clam broth through sieve lined with paper towels; set aside. When cool enough to handle, remove clams from shells and coarsely chop. Discard shells.

3. Meanwhile, in large saucepot, cook pasta as label directs. Drain.

4. Add oil, garlic, and crushed red pepper to same clean Dutch oven. Cook over medium heat, stirring occasionally, just until garlic turns golden. Stir in parsley, clams, and clam broth; heat just to simmering. Add pasta to Dutch oven and toss until combined.

EACH SERVING About 427 calories | 19g protein | 59g carbohydrate | 11g total fat (1g saturated) | 24mg cholesterol | 111mg sodium.

Linguine with Red Clam Sauce

If fresh clams or mussels aren't available, you can substitute two cans (ten ounces each) of whole baby clams plus one-fourth of the clam liquid for the littlenecks.

PREP 20 minutes **COOK** 1 hour **MAKES** 6 main-dish servings.

Marinara Sauce (page 72)

$^1/_2$ **cup dry white wine**

2 dozen littleneck clams, scrubbed

1 package (16 ounces) linguine

1 tablespoon butter or margarine, cut into pieces (optional)

$^1/_4$ **cup chopped fresh parsley**

1. Prepare Marinara Sauce.

2. In nonreactive 12-inch skillet, heat wine to boiling over high heat. Add clams; cover and cook until clams open, 5 to 10 minutes, transferring clams to bowl as they open. Discard any clams that have not opened. Strain clam broth through sieve lined with paper towels; reserve $^1/_4$ cup. When cool enough to handle, remove clams from shells and coarsely chop. Discard shells.

3. Meanwhile, in large saucepot, cook pasta as label directs. Drain.

4. In same clean 12-inch skillet, combine marinara sauce, reserved clam broth, and clams; cook over low heat until heated through. In warm serving bowl, toss pasta with sauce and butter, if using. Sprinkle with parsley and serve.

EACH SERVING About 429 calories | 20g protein | 67g carbohydrate | 9g total fat (2g saturated) | 29mg cholesterol | 582mg sodium.

Classic Lasagna with Meat Sauce

We call for no-boil noodles for this popular dish—they're a real time-saver. Layer them straight from the package with lots of sauce; as the lasagna bakes and absorbs the liquid, the pasta will soften and expand. If your package contains fifteen noodles, use an extra noodle in the first three layers when assembling the lasagna.

PREP 1 hour **BAKE** 30 minutes **MAKES** 10 main-dish servings.

MEAT SAUCE

8 ounces sweet Italian-sausage links, casings removed

8 ounces lean ground beef

1 small onion, finely chopped

2 garlic cloves, minced

1 can (28 ounces) plus 1 can (14 to 16 ounces) whole tomatoes in juice

2 tablespoons tomato paste

$^1/_2$ teaspoon salt

2 tablespoons chopped fresh basil leaves

CHEESE FILLING

1 large egg

$^1/_4$ teaspoon coarsely ground black pepper

1 container (15 ounces) part-skim ricotta cheese

4 ounces part-skim mozzarella cheese, shredded (1 cup)

$^3/_4$ cup freshly grated Parmesan cheese

1 package (8 ounces) no-boil lasagna noodles (12 noodles)

1. Prepare sauce: Heat 4-quart saucepan over medium-high heat until hot. Add sausage and ground beef and cook, stirring, 1 minute. Add onion and cook, stirring occasionally and breaking up sausage with side of spoon, until meat is browned and onion is tender, about 5 minutes. Pour off drippings from saucepan. Add garlic to meat mixture in saucepan and cook 1 minute.

2. Stir in tomatoes with their juice, tomato paste, and salt, breaking up tomatoes with side of spoon; heat to boiling. Reduce heat to medium and cook, uncovered and stirring occasionally, 20 minutes. Stir in basil. Makes about 6 cups sauce.

3. Meanwhile, prepare filling. In medium bowl, mix egg, pepper, ricotta, $^1/_2$ cup mozzarella, and $^1/_2$ cup Parmesan until blended.

4. Preheat oven to 350°F. In 13" by 9" glass baking dish, evenly spread 2 cups sauce. Arrange 3 noodles over sauce, making sure noodles do not touch sides of dish (they will expand). Top with $1^1/_2$ cups cheese filling, 3 noodles, and 2 cups sauce. Arrange 3 noodles over sauce; spread with remaining filling. Top with remaining noodles and remaining sauce. Sprinkle with remaining $^1/_2$ cup mozzarella and $^1/_4$ cup Parmesan. (If making a day ahead, cover and refrigerate.)

5. Cover lasagna with foil and bake until heated through and bubbling, about 30 minutes (1 hour if refrigerated). Let stand 10 minutes for easier serving.

EACH SERVING About 350 calories | 24g protein | 27g carbohydrate |
16g total fat (8g saturated) | 78mg cholesterol | 775mg sodium.

Meatballs and Old-Fashioned Tomato Sauce

Our recipe makes enough meatballs and sauce for twelve servings. So, make a batch to serve today, and still have enough to freeze for one or two more easy weeknight dinners.

PREP 35 minutes   COOK 50 minutes   MAKES 24 meatballs and 10 cups sauce.

MEATBALLS

$^1/_3$ cup water

4 slices firm white bread, coarsely grated

1 pound lean ground beef

1 pound lean ground turkey or lean ground pork

2 large egg whites

$^1/_3$ cup grated Romano or Parmesan cheese

1 garlic clove, crushed with garlic press

1 teaspoon salt

$^1/_4$ teaspoon coarsely ground black pepper

OLD-FASHIONED TOMATO SAUCE

2 tablespoons olive oil

3 medium carrots, peeled and finely chopped

2 medium onions, finely chopped

3 garlic cloves, crushed with garlic press

3 cans (28 ounces each) Italian-style plum tomatoes in puree

$^3/_4$ teaspoon salt

$^1/_4$ teaspoon coarsely ground black pepper

1. Preheat oven to 450°F.

2. Prepare meatballs: In large bowl, pour water over bread. With hands, toss until bread is evenly moistened. Add ground beef, ground turkey, egg whites, grated cheese, garlic, salt, and pepper; mix with hands just until evenly combined but not overmixed.

3. Shape meat mixture into twenty-four 2-inch meatballs, handling meat as little as possible (for easier shaping, use slightly wet hands). Arrange meatballs in 15$^1/_2$" by 10$^1/_2$" jelly-roll pan and bake until cooked through and lightly browned, 18 to 20 minutes.

4. Meanwhile, prepare Old-Fashioned Tomato Sauce: In 6-quart Dutch

oven or saucepot, heat oil over medium heat until hot. Add carrots and onions and cook until vegetables are tender and golden, about 15 minutes. Add garlic and cook, stirring, 1 minute.

5. Pour tomatoes with puree into large bowl. With hands, slotted spoon, or kitchen shears, break up tomatoes until well crushed. Add tomatoes with puree, salt, and pepper to vegetable mixture; heat to boiling over high heat, stirring occasionally. Reduce heat to medium; cover and cook 10 minutes. Add meatballs and cook, uncovered, stirring occasionally, 15 minutes longer. Makes enough meatballs and sauce for 3 pounds pasta.

EACH MEATBALL About 80 calories | 9g protein | 2g carbohydrate | 4g total fat (1g saturated) | 22mg cholesterol | 155mg sodium.

EACH ¼ CUP SAUCE About 25 calories | 1g protein | 4g carbohydrate | 1g total fat (0g saturated) | 0mg cholesterol | 250mg sodium.

GH Test Kitchen Tip: Grating Fresh Bread Crumbs

Grate firm day-old Italian or French bread on the large holes of a box grater. Or process the bread in a food processor with the knife blade attached to form coarse crumbs. One slice of bread yields about ½ cup crumbs.

Neapolitan Pasta Sauce

This is the kind of old-time pasta sauce that simmers for hours, filling the kitchen with enticing aromas. It makes a big batch, enough for about five pounds of pasta, so plan to freeze the leftovers. Serve with a sturdy pasta such as rigatoni. Top with freshly grated Pecorino Romano.

PREP 15 minutes   **COOK** 4 hours 15 minutes   **MAKES** 16 cups.

2 pounds boneless pork shoulder blade roast (fresh pork butt), trimmed

1 garlic clove, thinly sliced

1 tablespoon olive oil

1 pound sweet Italian-sausage links

8 ounces hot Italian-sausage links

2 large onions (12 ounces each), finely chopped

4 garlic cloves, finely chopped

4 cans (28 ounces each) plum tomatoes

1 can (28 ounces) tomato puree

1 tablespoon sugar

$^1/_2$ teaspoon salt

1. With small knife, make several slits in pork shoulder and insert garlic slices. In nonreactive 12-quart saucepot, heat oil over medium heat until very hot. Cook pork and sweet and hot sausages in batches until lightly browned, using slotted spoon to transfer meat to bowl as it is browned.

2. Add onions and chopped garlic to saucepot; cook until onion is tender, about 5 minutes. Add tomatoes with their juice, tomato puree, sugar, and salt; heat to boiling, breaking up tomatoes with side of spoon.

3. Return pork to saucepot. Reduce heat; partially cover and simmer 3 hours. Add sausage and cook until pork is very tender, about 45 minutes longer. Remove pork and cut into bite-size pieces; return to saucepot (keep sausages whole). Use 3 cups sauce to coat 1 pound pasta for 6 main-dish servings.

EACH $^1/_2$ **CUP** About 139 calories | 9g protein | 5g carbohydrate | 9g total fat (3g saturated) | 35mg cholesterol | 318mg sodium.

Classic Bolognese Sauce

A staple in Bologna, this tomato-based meat sauce, enriched with cream and mellowed by long simmering, is well worth the time. This recipe makes a generous amount of sauce. About two and a half cups is enough to coat a pound of pasta. Freeze leftovers in small batches.

PREP 10 minutes **COOK** 1 hour 25 minutes **MAKES** 5 cups.

2 tablespoons olive oil

1 medium onion, chopped

1 carrot, peeled and finely chopped

1 stalk celery, finely chopped

1^1/$_2$ pounds ground meat for meat loaf (beef, pork, and/or veal) or ground beef chuck

^{1}/$_2$ cup dry red wine

1 can (28 ounces) plum tomatoes, chopped

2 teaspoons salt

^{1}/$_4$ teaspoon ground black pepper

^{1}/$_8$ teaspoon ground nutmeg

^{1}/$_4$ cup heavy or whipping cream

1. In nonreactive 5-quart Dutch oven, heat oil over medium heat. Add onion, carrot, and celery and cook, stirring occasionally, until tender, about 10 minutes.

2. Add ground meat and cook, breaking up meat with side of spoon, until no longer pink. Stir in wine and heat to boiling. Stir in tomatoes with their juice, salt, pepper, and nutmeg. Heat to boiling over high heat. Reduce heat and simmer, stirring occasionally, 1 hour.

3. Stir in cream and heat through, stirring constantly. Use 2^1/$_2$ cups sauce to coat 1 pound pasta for 6 main-dish servings.

EACH SERVING About 678 calories | 32g protein | 68g carbohydrate | 30g total fat (11g saturated) | 104mg cholesterol | 1,210mg sodium.

Marinara Sauce

This sauce is very versatile. For a toothsome alternative, stir eight ounces of sweet or hot Italian-sausage links, cooked and crumbled, into the sauce. Or top each serving with a spoonful of ricotta cheese for a creamy treat.

PREP 5 minutes **COOK** 30 minutes **MAKES** 3 $\frac{1}{2}$ cups.

2 tablespoons olive oil

1 small onion, chopped

1 garlic clove, finely chopped

1 can (28 ounces) plum tomatoes

2 tablespoons tomato paste

2 tablespoons chopped fresh basil or parsley (optional)

$\frac{1}{2}$ teaspoon salt

1. In nonreactive 3-quart saucepan, heat oil over medium heat; add onion and garlic and cook, stirring, until onion is tender, about 5 minutes.

2. Stir in tomatoes with their juice, tomato paste, basil if using, and salt. Heat to boiling, breaking up tomatoes with side of spoon. Reduce heat; partially cover and simmer, stirring occasionally, until sauce has thickened slightly, about 20 minutes. Use to coat 1 pound pasta for 4 main-dish servings.

EACH $\frac{1}{2}$ **CUP** About 67 calories | 1g protein | 7g carbohydrate | 4g total fat (1g saturated) | 0mg cholesterol | 388mg sodium.

GH Test Kitchen Tip

Choose the right pasta for your sauce. While personal taste comes into play, here are some tried-and-true guidelines.

- Thin pastas, such as capellini and vermicelli, should be dressed with delicate, light sauces. Meat sauces tend to slip off the skinny strands and end up at the bottom of the bowl.
- Fettuccine and linguine are excellent with light-bodied meat, vegetable, seafood, cheese, and cream sauces.
- Tubular pastas are great with meat sauces: The nuggets of meat nestle right inside the tubes. Chunky vegetable or olive sauces are also a good match for macaroni-type pastas, as well as for baked dishes.
- Tiny pastas are best saved for soups or combined with other ingredients.

Asparagus Risotto

Sweet asparagus brings fresh spring flavor to this favorite rice dish.

PREP 15 minutes **COOK** 50 minutes **MAKES** 4 main-dish servings or about 8 cups

4 cups water

1 can (14^1/$_2$ ounces) chicken broth or vegetable broth

1^1/$_2$ pounds asparagus, trimmed

2 tablespoons margarine or butter

1 small onion, finely chopped

2 cups **Arborio rice** (Italian short-grain rice) or medium-grain rice

^{1}/$_2$ cup dry white wine

^{3}/$_4$ cup freshly grated Parmesan cheese

^{3}/$_4$ teaspoon salt

^{1}/$_4$ teaspoon ground black pepper

1. In 2-quart saucepan, heat water and broth to boiling over high heat. Reduce heat to maintain simmer; cover.

2. If using thin asparagus, cut each stalk crosswise in half and reserve halves with tips; if using medium asparagus, cut 1 inch from asparagus tops and reserve tips. Cut remaining asparagus stalks into ^{1}/$_4$-inch pieces.

3. In deep nonstick 12-inch skillet, melt 1 tablespoon margarine over medium heat. Add onion and asparagus pieces (not tips) and cook, stirring occasionally, until vegetables begin to soften, about 10 minutes.

4. Add rice and remaining 1 tablespoon margarine, and cook, stirring frequently, until rice grains are opaque. Add wine; cook, stirring, until wine has been absorbed.

5. Add about ^{1}/$_2$ cup simmering broth to rice, stirring until liquid has been absorbed. Continue cooking, adding remaining broth, ^{1}/$_2$ cup at a time and stirring after each addition, about 25 minutes. Stir in reserved asparagus tips with last ^{1}/$_2$ cup broth and cook until all liquid has been absorbed and rice and asparagus are tender (risotto should have a creamy consistency). Remove risotto from heat; stir in Parmesan, salt, and pepper.

EACH SERVING About 590 calories | 19g protein | 96g carbohydrate | 11g total fat (4g saturated) | 12mg cholesterol | 1,245mg sodium.

Risotto Milanese

Saffron-infused Risotto Milanese is the traditional accompaniment to Osso Buco (page 35). It is also delicious as a first course or as a meatless main course when followed by a generous mixed green salad.

PREP 10 minutes   **COOK** 45 minutes
MAKES 8 accompaniment servings or about 6½ cups.

3½ cups water

1 can (14½ ounces) chicken broth

2 tablespoons butter or olive oil

1 small onion, finely chopped

2 cups Arborio rice (Italian short-grain rice) or medium-grain rice

1 teaspoon salt

½ cup dry white wine

¼ teaspoon loosely packed saffron threads

½ cup freshly grated Parmesan cheese

1. In 2-quart saucepan, heat water and broth to boiling over high heat. Reduce heat to maintain simmer; cover.

2. In 4-quart saucepan, melt butter over medium heat. Add onion and cook, stirring occasionally, until tender, about 5 minutes. Add rice and salt and cook, stirring frequently, until rice grains are opaque. Add wine; cook, stirring, until wine has been absorbed.

3. Add about ½ cup simmering broth to rice, stirring until liquid has been absorbed. Continue cooking, adding broth ½ cup at a time and stirring

---

GH Test Kitchen Tip

Arborio is the traditional rice for Italian risotto; the plump roundish medium-grain rice has a high starch content and yields a moist, creamy texture. *Vialone Nano* and *Carnaroli* rice varieties can also be used to make risotto. They have a higher starch content than Arborio, which some cooks find preferable. Previously, only imported Arborio was available, now domestic varieties of Arborio are cultivated. Some imported varieties are simply labeled "short-grain" because the Italian government has only two rice categories—long and short.

---

after each addition. After cooking 10 minutes, crumble saffron into rice. Continue cooking, adding remaining broth $^1/_2$ cup at a time and stirring after each addition, until all liquid has been absorbed and rice is tender but still firm, about 25 minutes longer (risotto should have a creamy consistency). Remove risotto from heat; stir in Parmesan.

EACH SERVING About 216 calories | 6g protein | 35g carbohydrate | 6g total fat (3g saturated) | 13mg cholesterol | 649mg sodium.

Creamy Polenta

Polenta has long been a popular staple in Northern Italy and now Americans love it, too. Our method ensures lump-free results. Serve with your favorite roasted or grilled bird.

PREP 5 minutes   **COOK** 30 minutes   **MAKES** 8 accompaniment servings.

2 cups cold water

I teaspoon salt

1$^1/_2$ cups yellow cornmeal

4$^1/_2$ cups boiling water

$^1/_2$ cup freshly grated Parmesan cheese

4 tablespoons butter or margarine, cut into pieces

1. In 5-quart Dutch oven, combine cold water and salt. With wire whisk, gradually beat in cornmeal until smooth. Whisk in boiling water. Heat to boiling over high heat. Reduce heat to medium-low and cook, stirring frequently with wooden spoon, until mixture is very thick, 20 to 25 minutes.

2. Stir Parmesan and butter into polenta until butter has melted. Serve immediately.

EACH SERVING About 173 calories | 5g protein | 20g carbohydrate | 8g total fat (5g saturated) | 20mg cholesterol | 464mg sodium.

Tuscan White Beans with Sage

These flawlessly flavored beans are perfect with roast pork or a grilled steak.

PREP 15 minutes plus soaking beans   **BAKE** 45 to 60 minutes
MAKES 8 accompaniment servings or about 6 cups.

1 package (16 ounces) white kidney beans (cannellini), soaked and drained

3 slices bacon

2 small onions, very thinly sliced

4 garlic cloves, crushed with side of chef's knife

2 sprigs plus 2 teaspoons thinly sliced fresh sage leaves

1 bay leaf

3 tablespoons olive oil

2 teaspoons salt

$^1/_2$ teaspoon ground black pepper

1. Preheat oven to 325°F. In 5-quart Dutch oven, combine beans, bacon, onions, garlic, sage sprigs, bay leaf, oil, and enough *water* to cover by 2 inches; heat to boiling over high heat. Cover and place in oven. Bake until beans are tender but still retain their shape, 45 to 60 minutes.

2. Drain beans, reserving cooking liquid. Discard bacon, sage sprigs, and bay leaf. Return beans to pot and stir in sliced sage, salt, pepper, and $^1/_2$ cup to 1 cup bean cooking liquid until desired consistency. Spoon into serving bowl and serve hot, warm, or at room temperature.

EACH SERVING About 263 calories | 14g protein | 37g carbohydrate | 7g total fat (1g saturated) | 2mg cholesterol | 617mg sodium.

Eggs

Asparagus and Green Onion Frittata

Asparagus and Green Onion Frittata

Everyone loves a skillet omelet, especially when it's filled with bits of cream cheese and sautéed vegetables.

PREP 25 minutes **BAKE** 10 minutes **MAKES** 4 main-dish servings.

8 large eggs

$^1/_2$ cup whole milk

$^3/_4$ teaspoon salt

$^1/_8$ teaspoon ground black pepper

12 ounces asparagus, trimmed

1 tablespoon margarine or butter

1 bunch green onions, trimmed and chopped

2 ounces light cream cheese (Neufchâtel)

1. Preheat oven to 375°F. In medium bowl, with wire whisk, mix eggs, milk, $^1/_2$ teaspoon salt, and pepper; set aside. If using thin asparagus, cut stalks crosswise in half; if using medium asparagus, cut stalks into 1-inch pieces.

2. In oven-safe nonstick 10-inch skillet (if skillet is not oven-safe, wrap handle with double layer of foil), melt margarine over medium heat. Add asparagus and remaining $^1/_4$ teaspoon salt and cook, stirring often, 4 minutes for thin stalks or 6 minutes for medium-size stalks. Stir in green onions and cook, stirring occasionally, until vegetables are tender, 2 to 3 minutes longer.

3. Reduce heat to medium-low. Pour egg mixture over vegetables; drop scant teaspoonfuls of cream cheese on top of egg mixture. Cook, without stirring, until egg mixture begins to set around edge, 3 to 4 minutes.

4. Place skillet in oven; bake until frittata is set and knife inserted in center comes out clean, 10 to 12 minutes. To serve, loosen frittata from skillet and slide onto warm platter; cut into 4 wedges.

EACH SERVING About 250 calories | 17g protein | 6g carbohydrate | 18g total fat (6g saturated) | 440mg cholesterol | 680mg sodium.

Summer Squash and Potato Frittata with Sage

It takes just a bit of minced sage to jazz up a humble egg entrée.

PREP 50 minutes **BAKE** 15 minutes **MAKES** 6 main-dish servings.

I large all-purpose potato (8 ounces), peeled and cut into $^1/_2$-inch chunks

1$^1/_2$ teaspoons salt

2 tablespoons margarine or butter

I medium red onion, thinly sliced

2 garlic cloves, minced

I small yellow summer squash (about 4 ounces), cut into 2" by $^1/_4$" strips

I small zucchini (about 4 ounces), cut into 2" by $^1/_4$" strips

2 teaspoons minced fresh sage leaves

$^1/_4$ teaspoon coarsely ground black pepper

8 large eggs

2 teaspoons balsamic vinegar

1. Preheat oven to 350°F. In 2-quart saucepan, place potato, $^1/_2$ teaspoon salt, and enough *water* to cover; heat to boiling over high heat. Reduce heat to low; cover and simmer until tender, about 10 minutes. Drain.

2. In oven-safe nonstick 10-inch skillet (if skillet is not oven-safe wrap handle with a double layer of foil), melt margarine over medium heat. Add onion and cook, stirring occasionally, until very soft, about 12 minutes.

3. Stir in garlic; cook 1 minute. Add cooked potato, squash, zucchini, sage, pepper, and remaining 1 teaspoon salt and cook, stirring occasionally, until zucchini is tender and liquid has evaporated, about 12 minutes.

4. In medium bowl, with fork, beat eggs and vinegar. Pour egg mixture over vegetables and cook, over medium heat, covered, until mixture begins to set around edge, about 3 minutes.

5. Remove cover and place skillet in oven; bake until frittata is set, about 15 minutes. To serve, loosen frittata from skillet and slide onto warm platter; cut into 6 wedges.

EACH SERVING About 180 calories | 10g protein | 11g carbohydrate | 11g total fat (3g saturated) | 284mg cholesterol | 540mg sodium.

Eggs in Spicy Tomato Sauce

This classic dish pairs an easy tomato sauce with eggs poached in the sauce. A delicious one-skillet dish to add to your quick-cook repertoire.

PREP 15 minutes **COOK** 25 minutes **MAKES** 4 main-dish servings.

1 loaf (8 ounces) Italian bread

1 tablespoon olive oil

1 jumbo onion (1 pound), finely chopped

2 medium carrots, peeled and finely chopped

1 stalk celery, finely chopped

2 garlic cloves, crushed with garlic press

1 can (28 ounces) plum tomatoes

1/2 teaspoon salt

1/4 teaspoon crushed red pepper

1 tablespoon margarine or butter

8 large eggs

1/4 cup loosely packed fresh basil leaves, chopped

1. Trim ends from bread. (Reserve ends for another use.) Cut loaf on diagonal into 1-inch-thick slices. Toast bread slices; set aside.

2. In nonstick 12-inch skillet, heat oil over medium-high heat until hot. Add onion, carrots, celery, and garlic and cook, stirring occasionally, until vegetables are lightly browned, 12 to 15 minutes.

3. Stir in tomatoes with their juice, salt, and crushed red pepper, breaking up tomatoes with spoon; heat to boiling over medium-high heat. Reduce heat to low; simmer, stirring occasionally, 5 minutes. Stir in margarine.

4. Break 1 egg into a custard cup. With back of spoon, make small well in sauce and slip egg into well. Repeat with remaining eggs. Heat sauce to boiling over medium-high heat. Reduce heat to medium-low; cover skillet and simmer until egg whites are set and yolks begin to thicken or until desired doneness, 7 to 10 minutes.

5. To serve, place 1 bread slice in each of 4 large soup bowls. Spoon 2 eggs and some tomato sauce over each bread slice; sprinkle with basil. Serve with remaining bread.

EACH SERVING About 455 calories | 21g protein | 52g carbohydrate | 19g total fat (5g saturated) | 425mg cholesterol | 1,100mg sodium.

Vegetables & Salads

Baked Artichokes with Parmesan Stuffing

Baked Artichokes with Parmesan Stuffing

The simple bread stuffing, seasoned with **Parmesan cheese, anchovies, and pine nuts, is a classic match for artichokes. If serving as a first course, use six small artichokes.**

PREP 1 hour **BAKE** 15 minutes **MAKES** 4 main-dish servings.

4 large artichokes

1 lemon, cut in half

2 tablespoons fresh lemon juice

4 slices firm white bread,
  coarsely grated (page 69)

2 tablespoons olive oil

2 large garlic cloves, finely chopped

4 anchovy fillets, chopped

$^1/_2$ cup pine nuts (pignoli), lightly
  toasted, or walnuts, toasted and
  chopped

$^1/_3$ cup freshly grated Parmesan
  cheese

2 tablespoons chopped fresh parsley

$^1/_4$ teaspoon salt

$^3/_4$ cup chicken broth

1. Trim artichokes: Bend back outer green leaves from around base of artichoke and snap off. With kitchen shears, trim thorny tops from remaining outer leaves, rubbing all cut surfaces with lemon half to prevent browning. Lay artichoke on its side and cut off stem level with bottom of artichoke. Peel stem; place in bowl of cold water and juice of remaining lemon half. Cut 1 inch off top of artichoke; add artichoke to lemon water. Repeat with remaining artichokes.

2. In nonreactive 5-quart saucepot, heat *1 inch water* and 1 tablespoon lemon juice to boiling over high heat. Stand artichokes in boiling water; add stems and heat to boiling. Reduce heat; cover and simmer until knife inserted in bottom of artichoke goes in easily, 30 to 40 minutes. Drain. When cool enough to handle, pull out prickly center leaves from each artichoke and, with teaspoon, scrape out fuzzy choke (without cutting into heart) and discard. Finely chop stems.

3. Meanwhile, preheat oven to 400°F. Spread grated bread in jelly-roll pan. Place in oven and toast until golden, about 5 minutes.

4. In 1-quart saucepan, heat oil over medium heat. Add garlic and cook 1 minute. Add anchovies and cook, stirring, until garlic is golden and anchovies have almost dissolved.

5. In medium bowl, combine toasted bread, pine nuts, Parmesan, parsley, chopped artichoke stems, garlic mixture, salt, $1/4$ cup broth, and remaining 1 tablespoon lemon juice.

6. Pour remaining $1/2$ cup broth into 13" by 9" baking dish; stand artichokes in dish. Spoon bread mixture between artichoke leaves and into center cavities. Bake until stuffing is golden and artichokes are heated through, 15 to 20 minutes.

EACH SERVING About 359 calories | 17g protein | 35g carbohydrate | 20g total fat (4g saturated) | 9mg cholesterol | 934mg sodium.

GH Test Kitchen Tip: How to Eat an Artichoke

To eat an artichoke, starting at bottom of artichoke, pluck off leaves one by one. Dip leaves in broth and pull through your teeth, scraping out pulp. Discard leaves. When leaves are too small and thin to eat, pull them out to reveal fuzzy choke. With tip on spoon, scrape out choke and discard. Cut solid heart into chunks if you like before eating.

Roman Artichokes

Artichokes require a bit of preparation before they are cooked, but it is not as complicated as people think, and they are well worth the effort. This classic dish, called *carciofi alla romana*, is one of the most attractive and appetizing ways to serve one of Italy's favorite vegetables.

PREP 25 minutes plus cooling   **COOK** 40 minutes   **MAKES** 8 first-course servings

8 medium artichokes

1 large lemon, cut in half

$^1/_4$ cup extravirgin olive oil

6 large mint sprigs plus $^1/_2$ cup loosely packed fresh mint leaves, chopped

3 large garlic cloves, finely chopped

2 cups water

$^1/_2$ cup dry white wine

$^1/_2$ teaspoon salt

$^1/_4$ teaspoon ground black pepper

1. Trim artichokes: Bend back outer green leaves from around base of artichoke and snap off. With kitchen shears, trim thorny tops from remaining outer leaves, rubbing all cut surfaces with lemon half to prevent browning. Lay artichoke on its side and cut off stem level with bottom of artichoke. Peel stem; place in bowl of cold water and juice of remaining lemon half. Cut 1 inch off top of artichoke; add artichoke to lemon water. Repeat with remaining artichokes.

2. In nonreactive 8-quart saucepot, heat oil over medium heat until hot. Add mint sprigs and garlic and cook, stirring frequently, 3 minutes. Add water, wine, salt, and pepper; heat to boiling over high heat.

3. Reduce heat to medium. Place artichokes, stem sides down, and stems in boiling liquid in saucepot. Cover and cook until knife inserted in bottom of artichokes goes in easily, 30 to 40 minutes.

4. Transfer 1 artichoke and some cooking liquid into 8 shallow soup bowls; serve warm or cool to room temperature. Sprinkle with remaining chopped mint.

EACH SERVING About 127 calories | 5g protein | 15g carbohydrate | 7g total fat (1g saturated) | 0mg cholesterol | 263mg sodium.

Breaded Cauliflower

Susan Westmoreland, *Good Housekeeping* Food Director, recalls helping her grandmother bread and fry platters of this addictive treat for family gatherings. It's delicious as an appetizer or side dish.

PREP 30 minutes **COOK** 40 minutes **MAKES** 12 accompaniment servings.

2 medium heads cauliflower (about 3¼ pounds), cut into 3-inch flowerets

vegetable oil for frying

4 large eggs

¼ cup milk

1½ cups seasoned dried bread crumbs

⅓ cup grated Pecorino Romano Cheese

¼ teaspoon freshly ground black pepper

salt (optional)

1. In 8-quart saucepot with steamer basket, heat *1 inch water* to boiling over high heat. Add cauliflower and reduce heat to medium. Cover and steam just until tender, about 10 minutes. Rinse with cold running water to stop cooking; drain well.

2. In 4-quart saucepan, heat 1 inch vegetable oil over medium heat until hot (350° to 375°F on deep-frying thermometer).

3. Preheat oven to 200°F. In large bowl, with wire whisk, lightly beat eggs with milk. In another large bowl, combine bread crumbs, Pecorino, and pepper. With tongs, dip cauliflower in egg mixture, then in bread crumbs to coat. In small batches, fry cauliflower, turning once, until light golden, 3 to 5 minutes. With slotted spoon, transfer cauliflower to paper towels to drain. Place drained cauliflower on jelly-roll pan and keep warm in oven.

4. Repeat with remaining cauliflower. Just before serving, sprinkle with salt, if you like.

EACH SERVING About 135 calories | 7g protein | 16g carbohydrate | 6g total fat (1g saturated) | 75mg cholesterol | 470mg sodium.

Cauliflower with Golden Raisins and Pine Nuts

This Sicilian-inspired side dish has just a touch of anchovy for authentic flavor. If you prefer to omit the anchovy, add a little more salt.

PREP 20 minutes   **COOK** 18 minutes   **MAKES** 6 accompaniment servings.

1 large head cauliflower (2^1/$_2$ pounds), cut into 1^1/$_2$-inch flowerets

2^1/$_4$ teaspoons salt

2 tablespoons olive oil

2 garlic cloves, crushed with side of chef's knife

1 teaspoon anchovy paste (optional)

^{1}/$_4$ teaspoon crushed red pepper

^{1}/$_4$ cup golden raisins

2 tablespoons pine nuts (pignoli), lightly toasted

1 tablespoon chopped fresh parsley

1. In 5-quart Dutch oven, heat *8 cups water* to boiling over high heat. Add cauliflower and 2 teaspoons salt; heat to boiling. Cook until tender, 5 to 7 minutes; drain. Wipe Dutch oven dry.

2. In same Dutch oven, heat oil over medium heat. Add garlic and cook until golden. Add anchovy paste, if using, and crushed red pepper; cook 15 seconds. Add cauliflower, raisins, pine nuts, and remaining ^{1}/$_4$ teaspoon salt; cook, stirring, until heated through, about 2 minutes. To serve, sprinkle with parsley.

EACH SERVING About 93 calories | 2g protein | 9g carbohydrate | 6g total fat (1g saturated) | 0mg cholesterol | 401mg sodium.

Caponata

Caponata (which gets its name from the capers in the dish) has an intriguing sweet-and-sour flavor. Serve it as part of a cold antipasto, spread it on bruschetta, or serve it on the side with grilled meat or poultry.

PREP 30 minutes plus cooling **ROAST/COOK** 45 minutes **MAKES** about 5 cups.

2 small eggplants (1 pound each), ends trimmed and cut into $^3/_4$-inch pieces

$^1/_2$ cup extravirgin olive oil

$^1/_4$ teaspoon salt

3 small red onions, thinly sliced

1$^1/_2$ pounds ripe tomatoes (4 medium), peeled, seeded, and chopped

1 cup olives, such as Gaeta, green Sicilian, or Kalamata, pitted and chopped

3 tablespoons capers, drained

3 tablespoons golden raisins

$^1/_4$ teaspoon coarsely ground black pepper

4 stalks celery with leaves, thinly sliced

$^1/_3$ cup red wine vinegar

2 teaspoons sugar

$^1/_4$ cup chopped fresh flat-leaf parsley

1. Preheat oven to 450°F. In two jelly-roll pans, place eggplant, dividing evenly. Drizzle with $^1/_4$ cup oil and sprinkle with salt; toss to coat. Roast eggplant 10 minutes, stir, and then roast until browned, about 10 minutes longer.

2. Meanwhile, in nonstick 12-inch skillet, heat remaining $^1/_4$ cup oil over medium heat. Add onions and cook, stirring, until tender and golden, about 10 minutes. Add tomatoes, olives, capers, raisins, and pepper. Reduce heat; cover and simmer 15 minutes.

3. Add eggplant and celery to skillet and cook over medium heat, stirring, until celery is just tender, 8 to 10 minutes. Stir in vinegar and sugar and cook 1 minute longer. Cool to room temperature, or cover and refrigerate up to overnight. To serve, sprinkle with parsley.

EACH $^1/_4$ **CUP About 106 calories | 1g protein | 9g carbohydrate | 8g total fat (1g saturated) | 0mg cholesterol | 336mg sodium.**

Escarole with Raisins and Pignoli

Sweet raisins balance the flavor of slightly bitter escarole.

PREP 10 minutes **COOK** 20 minutes **MAKES** 4 accompaniment servings.

1 tablespoon olive oil	$1/4$ cup golden raisins
1 garlic clove, finely chopped	$1/4$ teaspoon salt
1 large head escarole (1 pound), coarsely chopped	2 tablespoons pine nuts (pignoli), toasted

In 5-quart Dutch oven, heat oil over medium heat. Stir in garlic and cook just until golden, about 30 seconds. Stir in escarole, raisins, and salt. Cover and cook 5 minutes. Remove cover and cook until escarole is tender and liquid has evaporated, about 10 minutes longer. Stir in pine nuts and remove from heat.

EACH SERVING About 101 calories | 3g protein | 12g carbohydrate | 6g total fat (1g saturated) | 0mg cholesterol | 169mg sodium.

Braised Fennel with Parmesan

Easy enough for a weeknight yet elegant enough for company.

PREP 15 minutes **BAKE** 1 hour **MAKES** 6 accompaniment servings.

3 medium fennel bulbs
  (1 pound each)

1 wedge Parmesan cheese

²/₃ cup chicken broth

¹/₃ cup water

1 tablespoon butter or margarine,
  cut into pieces

¹/₈ teaspoon coarsely ground
  black pepper

1. Preheat oven to 425°F.

2. Trim fronds from fennel, if attached. Rinse fennel under cold running water. Trim root end and remove stalks. Cut bulb lengthwise into ¹/₂-inch-thick slices.

3. With vegetable peeler, remove enough shavings from wedge of Parmesan to measure ¹/₂ cup, loosely packed (about 1 ounce).

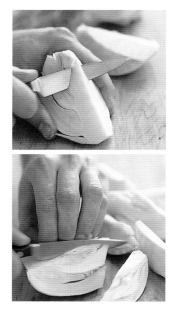

4. Place fennel in 13" by 9" baking dish. Pour broth and water over fennel and top with butter. Cover with foil. Bake 15 minutes. Remove foil; turn fennel and bake, uncovered, until very tender and liquid has almost been absorbed, 40 to 45 minutes.

5. Arrange Parmesan shavings over fennel and sprinkle with pepper. Bake until Parmesan melts, about 5 minutes longer.

EACH SERVING About 106 calories | 8g protein | 6g carbohydrate | 6g total fat (4g saturated) | 15mg cholesterol | 540mg sodium.

Stuffed Italian Frying Peppers

Serve these peppers as part of an antipasto platter or Mediterranean-inspired buffet, hot or at room temperature. This recipe is easily doubled.

PREP 35 minutes **BAKE** 45 minutes **MAKES** 4 accompaniment servings.

2 cups fresh $1/2$-inch bread cubes (about 3 slices bread)

2 tablespoons olive oil

1 medium onion, chopped

2 garlic cloves, finely chopped

$3/4$ cup freshly grated Pecorino Romano cheese

$1/3$ cup chopped fresh parsley

4 Italian frying peppers (3 ounces each), tops removed and seeded

1. Preheat oven to 375°F. On cookie sheet, toast bread cubes until light golden, about 7 minutes.

2. Meanwhile, in 10-inch skillet, heat 1 tablespoon oil over medium heat. Add onion and garlic and cook, stirring, until tender, about 5 minutes. Transfer to large bowl.

3. Add cheese, parsley, and croutons to onion, tossing to combine. Spoon crouton mixture into peppers, pressing down gently to fill. Place peppers on their sides in 11" by 7" baking dish. Drizzle remaining 1 tablespoon oil over peppers and cover with foil. Bake 40 minutes. Remove foil and bake until peppers are tender, about 5 minutes longer.

EACH SERVING About 211 calories | 9g protein | 19g carbohydrate | 12g total fat (4g saturated) | 15mg cholesterol | 282mg sodium.

Sautéed Spinach and Garlic

In just five minutes, you'll have a satisfying side dish. To save time, use bags of prewashed baby spinach.

PREP 15 minutes   **COOK** 5 minutes   **MAKES** 4 accompaniment servings.

1 tablespoon vegetable oil

2 garlic cloves, crushed with side of chef's knife

2 bunches (10 to 12 ounces each) spinach, washed and dried very well, tough stems trimmed

¼ teaspoon salt

In 5-quart Dutch oven, heat oil over medium-high heat. Add garlic and cook, stirring, until golden. Add spinach in batches; add salt. Cover and cook, stirring once, just until spinach wilts, about 4 minutes. Discard garlic, if you like.

EACH SERVING About 57 calories | 3g protein | 4g carbohydrate | 4g total fat (0g saturated) | 0mg cholesterol | 232mg sodium.

Venetian-Style Zucchini

This traditional method of preparing vegetables is called *agrodolce* (literally, "sweet and sour") in Italy. Thin zucchini slices are fried in oil, then marinated in a mint, raisin, and balsamic vinegar mixture.

PREP 20 minutes plus standing **COOK** 6 minutes per batch
MAKES 6 accompaniment servings.

3 tablespoons golden raisins

3 tablespoons balsamic vinegar

1 tablespoon minced fresh mint

1 teaspoon dark brown sugar

$1/2$ teaspoon salt

$1/8$ teaspoon ground black pepper

1 garlic clove, peeled and cut in half

vegetable oil for frying

8 small zucchini (about 5 ounces each), cut crosswise into $1/4$-inch-thick slices

1 tablespoon pine nuts (pignoli), toasted

mint sprigs

1. In large bowl, combine raisins, vinegar, mint, brown sugar, salt, pepper, and garlic; stir until mixed. Set aside.

2. In 10-inch skillet, heat $1/2$ inch oil over medium-high heat until hot but not smoking. Add 2 cups zucchini; fry until golden, 6 to 8 minutes. With slotted spoon, transfer cooked zucchini to coarse sieve; let drain. While still hot, stir zucchini into vinegar mixture.

3. Repeat with remaining zucchini in batches of 2 cups each. Let stand at room temperature at least 1 hour.

4. Cover and refrigerate for up to 3 days, if you like. Serve at room temperature, topped with pine nuts and mint sprigs.

EACH SERVING About 140 calories | 3g protein | 12g carbohydrate | 10g total fat (1g saturated) | 0mg cholesterol | 185mg sodium.

Ciambotta

As with many vegetable stews, the ingredients for ciambotta can be varied according to what you have on hand and the flavors you prefer. It can also be served at room temperature.

PREP 30 minutes **COOK** 30 minutes **MAKES** 6 accompaniment servings.

3 tablespoons olive oil

1 medium onion, chopped

2 garlic cloves, finely chopped

2 red peppers, cut into 1-inch pieces

1½ pounds zucchini (3 medium),
  cut lengthwise in half, then into
  ½-inch pieces

1½ pounds ripe tomatoes, peeled,
  seeded, and chopped

¾ teaspoon salt

⅓ cup chopped fresh basil

1. In nonreactive 12-inch skillet, heat 2 tablespoons oil over medium heat. Add onion and garlic and cook, stirring frequently, until onion is tender, about 5 minutes. Add red peppers and cook, stirring frequently, until red peppers are tender-crisp, about 5 minutes longer.

2. Add remaining 1 tablespoon oil and zucchini; cook, stirring, until zucchini are tender-crisp, about 5 minutes. Add tomatoes and salt; heat to boiling. Reduce heat; cover and simmer until vegetables are very tender, about 10 minutes. Stir in basil.

EACH SERVING About 117 calories | 3g protein | 13g carbohydrate | 7g total fat (1g saturated) | 0mg cholesterol | 305mg sodium.

Easy Tomato and Mozzarella Salad

Toss farm-stand tomatoes (we love to use red, yellow, and orange) with basil and extravirgin olive oil for one of summer's simplest pleasures. For the best flavor, don't refrigerate this salad.

PREP 20 minutes **MAKES** 8 accompaniment servings.

3 pounds tomatoes, cut into 1¹/₂-inch chunks

8 ounces lightly salted, small fresh mozzarella balls, each cut in half, or 1 package (8 ounces) mozzarella cheese, cut into ¹/₂-inch chunks

1 cup loosely packed fresh basil leaves, chopped

3 tablespoons extravirgin olive oil

³/₄ teaspoon salt

¹/₄ teaspoon coarsely ground black pepper

In large bowl, toss tomatoes, mozzarella, basil, oil, salt, and pepper until well mixed.

EACH SERVING About 160 calories | 7g protein | 9g carbohydrate | 12g total fat (5g saturated) | 22mg cholesterol | 255mg sodium.

Panzanella Salad with Tomato Vinaigrette

This classic Italian bread salad depends on a hearty loaf that won't get mushy when mixed with moist ingredients. We toss ours with a homemade tomato vinaigrette for the most flavor.

PREP 35 minutes   **COOK** 15 minutes   **MAKES** 6 main-dish servings.

4 ounces pancetta or 4 slices bacon, cut into $1/4$-inch pieces

1 tablespoon olive oil

1 small loaf (6 ounces) crusty peasant or sourdough bread, cut into $1/2$-inch cubes

Tomato Vinaigrette (page 98)

2 tablespoons freshly grated Parmesan cheese

$1/4$ teaspoon ground black pepper

4 small bunches arugula (4 ounces each), trimmed

$1 1/2$ pints red and/or yellow cherry tomatoes, cut in half

1. In nonstick 12-inch skillet, cook pancetta over medium heat until lightly browned. With slotted spoon, transfer to large serving bowl.

2. To pancetta drippings in skillet, add oil and bread cubes; cook, stirring occasionally, until bread cubes are lightly browned, about 10 minutes.

3. Meanwhile, prepare Tomato Vinaigrette.

4. Add croutons, Parmesan, and pepper to pancetta in bowl and toss to combine. Add arugula and cherry tomatoes to croutons in bowl. Add Tomato Vinaigrette; toss until mixed and coated with dressing.

EACH SERVING About 246 calories | 8g protein | 21g carbohydrate | 15g total fat (4g saturated) | 13mg cholesterol | 562mg sodium.

Tomato Vinaigrette

This summer's-end salad dressing starts with a ripe tomato, which gives the dressing body and richness. It's perfect in **Panzanella Salad** or spooned over sliced tomatoes and feta cheese, spinach salad, or mixed greens.

PREP 15 minutes **MAKES** about 1 cup.

1 small tomato (4 ounces), peeled and coarsely chopped

1 small shallot, cut in half

2 tablespoons olive oil

1 tablespoon red wine vinegar

1 tablespoon balsamic vinegar

2 teaspoons Dijon mustard with seeds

1 teaspoon chopped fresh oregano

1 teaspoon sugar

$^1/_4$ teaspoon salt

$^1/_4$ teaspoon ground black pepper

In blender, combine tomato, shallot, oil, red wine and balsamic vinegars, mustard, oregano, sugar, salt, and pepper; puree just until smooth. Transfer to bowl or jar. Cover and refrigerate up to 1 day.

EACH SERVING About 19 calories | 0g protein | 1g carbohydrate | 2g total fat (0g saturated) | 0mg cholesterol | 51mg sodium.

Fennel Salad with Olives and Mint

Serve at lunch with bread, cheese, and salami or as a side dish with fish or roasted chicken.

PREP 20 minutes   **MAKES** 6 accompaniment servings.

1 large lemon

2 medium fennel bulbs, trimmed and sliced lengthwise into thin strips (about 4 cups), plus 1 tablespoon minced fennel fronds

$^1/_4$ cup chopped red onion

$^3/_4$ cup **Mediterranean-style green olives, pitted and finely chopped**

1 cup loosely packed fresh mint leaves, minced

3 tablespoons olive oil

$^1/_2$ teaspoon salt

$^1/_8$ teaspoon ground black pepper

1. From lemon, grate 2 teaspoons peel and squeeze 3 tablespoons juice.

2. In large bowl, toss fennel, onion, olives, mint, oil, lemon peel and juice, salt, and pepper until well mixed. Cover and refrigerate if not serving right away.

EACH SERVING About 95 calories | 1g protein | 6g carbohydrate | 9g total fat (1g saturated) | 0mg cholesterol | 460mg sodium.

Italian Seafood Salad

Italians serve this salad on **Christmas Eve** along with other fish dishes, and enjoy it throughout the year as a refreshing first course.

PREP 50 minutes plus chilling   **COOK** 15 minutes   **MAKES** 12 first-course servings.

1 pound sea scallops

2 pounds cleaned squid

1 small lemon, thinly sliced

2 pounds large shrimp, shelled and deveined

²/₃ cup fresh lemon juice (4 lemons)

¹/₂ cup olive oil

1 small garlic clove, minced

¹/₂ teaspoon coarsely ground black pepper

4 large stalks celery, cut into ¹/₂-inch pieces

¹/₂ cup Gaeta or Niçoise olives (optional)

¹/₄ cup loosely packed fresh parsley leaves

1. Pull off and discard tough crescent-shaped muscle from each scallop. Rinse squid; slice bodies crosswise into ³/₄-inch-thick rings. Cut tentacles into several pieces if large. In 5-quart Dutch oven, combine *2¹/₂ inches water* and lemon slices; heat to boiling over high heat. Add shrimp. Reduce heat to medium; cook until shrimp are opaque throughout, 1 to 2 minutes. With slotted spoon, transfer shrimp to colander to drain; transfer to large serving bowl.

2. To boiling water in Dutch oven, add scallops; cook just until opaque throughout, 2 to 3 minutes. With slotted spoon, transfer to colander to drain; add to shrimp in bowl.

3. To boiling water in Dutch oven, add squid; cook until tender and opaque, 30 seconds to 1 minute. Drain in colander; add to shrimp and scallops in bowl.

4. Prepare dressing: In small bowl, with wire whisk, mix lemon juice, oil, garlic, and pepper until blended. Add celery, olives if using, and parsley to seafood in bowl; toss to mix. Add dressing and toss until mixed and coated with dressing. Cover and refrigerate salad at least 3 hours to blend flavors or up to 8 hours.

EACH SERVING About 255 calories | 31g protein | 6g carbohydrate | 11g total fat (2g saturated) | 282mg cholesterol | 200mg sodium.

Breads, Pizza & Sandwiches

Focaccia
recipe on page 106

Breadsticks

These breadsticks keep perfectly for up to a week in an airtight container.

PREP 40 minutes plus resting BAKE 20 minutes per batch MAKES 64 breadsticks.

2 packages quick-rise yeast

2¹/₂ teaspoons salt

about 4³/₄ cups all-purpose flour

1¹/₃ cups very warm water
  (120° to 130°F)

¹/₂ cup olive oil

3 tablespoons caraway seeds, or
  sesame seeds, poppy seeds, or
  freshly grated Parmesan cheese

1. In large bowl, combine yeast, salt, and 2 cups flour. With wooden spoon, stir in very warm water; beat vigorously 1 minute. Stir in oil. Gradually stir in 2¹/₄ cups flour. Stir in caraway seeds, if using.

2. Turn dough onto lightly floured surface and knead until smooth and elastic, about 8 minutes, working in enough of remaining ¹/₂ cup flour just to keep dough from sticking. Cover dough loosely with plastic wrap; let rest 10 minutes.

3. Preheat oven to 375°F. Grease two large cookie sheets. Cut dough in half. Cover one dough half; cut remaining dough half into 32 equal pieces. Shape each piece into 12-inch-long rope. Place ropes, 1 inch apart, on prepared cookie sheets. If not using caraway seeds, sprinkle with sesame seeds, poppy seeds, or Parmesan.

4. Bake breadsticks until golden and crisp, about 20 minutes, rotating cookie sheets between upper and lower oven racks halfway through baking. Transfer to wire racks to cool. Repeat with remaining dough.

EACH BREADSTICK About 52 calories | 1g protein | 7g carbohydrate | 2g total fat (0g saturated) | 0mg cholesterol | 91mg sodium.

Rosemary-Fennel Breadsticks

Prepare as directed but omit caraway, sesame, or poppy seeds or Parmesan. In Step 1, stir **2 teaspoons fennel seeds**, crushed, **1 teaspoon dried rosemary leaves**, crumbled, and ¹/₂ **teaspoon coarsely ground black pepper** into dough. Proceed as directed.

Ciabatta

Try this crusty bread with any hearty soup or stew. We also like it with a simple green salad.

PREP 30 minutes plus rising **BAKE** 25 minutes **MAKES** 2 loaves, 12 slices each.

1 package active dry yeast	1 tablespoon salt
1 teaspoon sugar	2 tablespoons milk
2¼ cups warm water (105° to 115° F)	2 tablespoons extravirgin olive oil
5 cups all-purpose flour	

1. In cup, combine yeast, sugar, and ¼ cup warm water; stir to disolve. Let stand until foamy, about 5 minutes.

2. In large bowl of heavy-duty mixer, combine flour and salt. With wooden spoon, stir in milk, oil, yeast mixture, and remaining 2 cups warm water until blended. With mixer at medium speed, beat until dough becomes elastic, about 15 minutes. (Or, if you prefer to mix by hand, combine ingredients as directed and stir with wooden spoon until dough becomes elastic, 15 minutes.) Dough will be very sticky and moist; do not add more flour and do not knead or stir for less than the suggested time.

3. Shape dough into ball; place in greased large bowl, turning dough to grease top. Cover bowl with plastic wrap and let rise in warm place (80° to 85°F) until doubled in volume, 1 hour to 1 hour and 30 minutes.

4. Flour large cookie sheet. With floured hands, punch down dough and divide in half. Place both pieces of dough on cookie sheet, about 3 inches apart; cover loosely with plastic wrap and let rest 15 minutes for easier shaping.

5. With hands, pull one piece of dough into 14" by 4" oval. Repeat with remaining piece of dough, keeping loaves 3 inches apart. With floured fingertips, make deep indentations, 1 inch apart, over entire surface of dough, almost to bottom of cookie sheet. Sprinkle lightly with flour. Cover loosely with plastic wrap and let rise in warm place until doubled, about 30 minutes.

6. Preheat oven to 425°F. Place 12 ice cubes in 13" by 9" metal baking pan. Place pan in bottom of oven. Bake ciabatta on middle rack until golden, 25 to 30 minutes, misting with water three times during first 10 minutes of baking. Transfer loaves to wire racks to cool.

EACH SLICE **About 105 calories** | **3g protein** | **20g carbohydrate** |
1g total fat (0g saturated) | **0mg cholesterol** | **270mg sodium.**

Focaccia

This bread's wonderfully chewy texture and fine crumb are due to three risings. Sprinkle either two tablespoons chopped fresh sage or one tablespoon chopped fresh rosemary over the focaccia just before baking, if you wish. (See photo on page 101.)

PREP 25 minutes plus rising   **BAKE** 18 minutes   **MAKES** 1 loaf, 12 slices.

1^1/$_2$ cups warm water (105° to 115°F)

1 package active dry yeast

1 teaspoon sugar

5 tablespoons extravirgin olive oil

1^1/$_2$ teaspoons table salt

3^3/$_4$ cups all-purpose flour or 3^1/$_2$ cups bread flour

1 teaspoon kosher salt or coarse sea salt

1. In large bowl, combine ^{1}/$_2$ cup warm water, yeast, and sugar; stir to dissolve. Let stand until foamy, about 5 minutes. Add remaining 1 cup warm water, 2 tablespoons oil, table salt, and flour; stir to combine.

2. Turn dough onto floured surface and knead until smooth and elastic, about 7 minutes. Dough will be soft; do not add more flour.

3. Shape dough into ball; place in greased large bowl, turning dough to grease top. Cover bowl with plastic wrap and let stand in warm place (80° to 85°F) until doubled in volume, about 1 hour.

4. Lightly oil 15^1/$_2$" by 10^1/$_2$" jelly-roll pan. Punch dough down and pat into prepared pan. Cover with plastic wrap and let rise in warm place until doubled, about 45 minutes.

5. With fingertips, make deep indentations, 1 inch apart, over entire surface of dough, almost to bottom of pan. Drizzle with remaining 3 tablespoons oil; sprinkle with kosher salt. Cover loosely with plastic wrap; let rise in warm place until doubled, about 45 minutes.

6. Preheat oven to 450°F. Bake focaccia on lowest oven rack until bottom is crusty and top is lightly browned, about 18 minutes. Transfer focaccia to wire rack to cool.

EACH SLICE About 201 calories | 4g protein | 31g carbohydrate | 7g total fat (1g saturated) | 0mg cholesterol | 537mg sodium.

Red Pepper Focaccia

Prepare as directed but do not sprinkle with kosher salt. In 12-inch skillet, heat **1 tablespoon olive oil** over medium heat. Add **4 red peppers,** sliced, and **1/4 teaspoon salt** and cook, stirring frequently, until tender, about 20 minutes. Cool to room temperature. Sprinkle over focaccia just before baking.

Dried Tomato and Olive Focaccia

Prepare as directed but do not sprinkle with kosher salt. Combine **1/2 cup Gaeta olives,** pitted, **1/4 cup drained oil-packed dried tomatoes,** coarsely chopped, and **1 1/2 teaspoons kosher salt.** Sprinkle over focaccia just before baking.

Onion Focaccia

Prepare as directed but do not sprinkle with kosher salt. In 12-inch skillet, heat **2 teaspoons olive oil** over medium heat. Add **2 medium onions,** sliced, **1 teaspoon sugar,** and **1/2 teaspoon salt** and cook, stirring frequently, until golden brown, about 20 minutes. Cool to room temperature. Spread over focaccia just before baking.

Semolina Focaccia

Patent durum or semolina flour is a high-protein, high-gluten flour milled from durum wheat. It is available in Italian grocery stores.

PREP 20 minutes plus rising **BAKE** 20 minutes **MAKES** 1 loaf, 12 slices.

1 package active dry yeast

6 tablespoons olive oil

1 teaspoon plus 2 tablespoons sugar

1 cup warm water (105° to 115°F)

2 teaspoons salt

1^1/$_2$ cups plus 2 tablespoons patent durum or finely ground semolina flour

about 1^1/$_2$ cups all-purpose flour

^{3}/$_4$ cup golden raisins

1 tablespoon fennel seeds, crushed

1. In cup, combine yeast, 3 tablespoons oil, 1 teaspoon sugar, and warm water; stir to dissolve. Let stand until foamy, about 5 minutes.

2. Meanwhile, in large bowl, combine remaining 2 tablespoons sugar, salt, 1^1/$_2$ cups patent durum flour, and 1^1/$_2$ cups all-purpose flour; stir to blend. With wooden spoon, stir in yeast mixture. With floured hands, knead until combined.

3. Turn dough onto lightly floured surface and knead until smooth and elastic, about 8 minutes, working in enough all-purpose flour (about 3 tablespoons) just to keep dough from sticking. Knead in raisins and fennel seeds.

4. Shape dough into ball; place in greased large bowl, turning dough to grease top. Cover bowl with plastic wrap and let stand in warm place (80° to 85°F) until doubled in volume, about 40 minutes.

5. Grease 15^1/$_2$" by 10^1/$_2$" jelly-roll pan; sprinkle with remaining 2 tablespoons patent durum flour. Punch dough down and place in prepared pan. With floured rolling pin, roll dough to even thickness in jelly-roll pan; press dough into corners with fingers. Cover with plastic wrap and let rise in warm place until doubled, about 30 minutes.

6. Preheat oven to 425°F. With fingertips, make deep indentations, about 1 inch apart, over entire surface of dough, almost to bottom of pan. Drizzle with remaining 3 tablespoons oil.

7. Bake focaccia on lowest rack until bottom is crusy and top is golden, about 20 minutes. Transfer focaccia to wire rack to cool.

EACH SLICE **About 240 calories** | **5g protein** | **40g carbohydrate** | **7g total fat (1g saturated)** | **0mg cholesterol** | **360mg sodium.**

GH Test Kitchen Tip

If you like, make our recipe in a bread machine to effortlessly produce a loaf with the same savory flavor, if not the shape, of this beloved Italian-style classic. For the bread-machine version, add the ingredients to the pan in the order specified by your machine's instruction manual but use only 1 1/2 cups patent durum or semolina flour, increase olive oil in dough to 1/4 cup, and don't drizzle bread with oil.

Tomato Focaccia

The dough for this popular Italian bread is "dimpled" (indented) just before baking. The dimples catch some of the olive oil drizzled on at the end for added flavor.

PREP 20 minutes plus rising **BAKE** 35 minutes **MAKES** 1 loaf, 12 slices.

1 package quick-rise yeast

about 4 cups all-purpose flour

2 teaspoons salt

6 tablespoons olive oil

1 1/3 cups water

1 tablespoon cornmeal

1 pound ripe plum tomatoes (about 5 medium), cut into 1/4-inch-thick slices

1 tablespoon chopped fresh rosemary or 1 teaspoon dried rosemary leaves, crushed

1/2 teaspoon coarsely ground black pepper

1. In large bowl, combine yeast, $1^{1}/_{2}$ cups flour, and $1^{1}/_{2}$ teaspoons salt.

2. In 1-quart saucepan, heat 4 tablespoons olive oil and water over medium heat until very warm (120° to 130°F).

3. With mixer at low speed, add liquid to dry ingredients and beat just until blended. Increase speed to medium; beat 2 minutes, scraping bowl often with rubber spatula. Add $^{1}/_{2}$ cup flour; beat 2 minutes. With spoon, stir in $1^{1}/_{2}$ cups flour. Dough will be soft.

4. Turn dough onto lightly floured surface and knead with floured hands, about 8 minutes, working in more flour (about $^{1}/_{2}$ cup). Cover dough with plastic wrap and let rest 15 minutes.

5. Grease $15^{1}/_{2}$" by $10^{1}/_{2}$" jelly-roll pan; sprinkle with cornmeal. Pat dough evenly into prepared pan. Cover with plastic wrap and let rise in warm place (80° to 85°F) until doubled in volume, about 30 minutes.

6. Preheat oven to 400°F. With fingertips, make deep indentations, 1 inch apart, over entire surface of dough, almost to bottom of pan. Drizzle with 1 tablespoon olive oil. Arrange sliced tomatoes over top; sprinkle with chopped rosemary, pepper, and remaining ¹/₂ teaspoon salt.

7. Bake focaccia in top third of oven until top is lightly browned, 35 to 40 minutes. Transfer focaccia to wire rack to cool; drizzle with remaining 1 tablespoon oil. Serve warm.

EACH SLICE **About 225 calories** I **5g protein** I **35g carbohydrate** I
7g total fat (1g saturated) I **0mg cholesterol** I **360mg sodium.**

Olive-Rosemary Loaves

Kalamata olives and fresh rosemary give this peasant loaf robust flavor. Using high-gluten bread flour guarantees your baking success.

PREP 30 minutes plus rising   **BAKE** 30 minutes   **MAKES** 2 loaves, 12 slices each.

1 1/2 cups warm water (105° to 115°F)

4 tablespoons extravirgin olive oil

2 packages active dry yeast

1 tablespoon sugar

1 cup Kalamata or green olives, pitted and chopped

2 tablespoons finely chopped fresh rosemary

2 teaspoons salt

about 5 cups bread flour or 5 1/4 cups all-purpose flour

1. In large bowl, combine 1/2 cup warm water, 3 tablespoons oil, yeast, and sugar; stir to dissolve. Let stand until foamy, about 5 minutes. Stir in remaining 1 cup warm water, olives, rosemary, salt, and 4 cups flour until combined.

2. Turn dough onto lightly floured surface and knead until smooth and elastic, about 8 minutes, working in enough of remaining flour just to keep dough from sticking.

3. Shape dough into ball; place in greased large bowl, turning dough to grease top. Cover bowl and let dough rise in warm place (80° to 85°F) until doubled in volume, about 1 hour.

4. Punch down dough. Turn dough onto lightly floured surface and cut in half; cover and let rest 15 minutes for easier shaping. Grease large cookie sheet.

5. Shape each dough half into 7 1/2" by 4" oval; place 3 inches apart on prepared cookie sheet. Cover and let rise in warm place until doubled, about 1 hour.

6. Meanwhile, preheat oven to 400°F. Brush tops of loaves with remaining 1 tablespoon oil. With serrated knife or single-edge razor blade, cut three diagonal slashes across top of each loaf. Bake until golden and loaves sound hollow when tapped on bottom, about 30 minutes. Cool on wire rack.

EACH SLICE About 148 calories | 4g protein | 23g carbohydrate | 4g total fat (1g saturated) | 0mg cholesterol | 296mg sodium.

Basic Pizza Dough

This recipe makes enough dough for two pizzas. If you like, freeze one ball for another time, perhaps to serve small wedges as appetizers. All-purpose flour makes a light crust, while bread flour gives it a chewy texture.

PREP 40 minutes plus rising **BAKE** 15 minutes
MAKES enough dough for 2 large pizzas, 4 main-dish servings each.

1 1/4 cups warm water (105° to 115°F)

1 package active dry yeast

1 teaspoon sugar

2 tablespoons olive oil

2 teaspoons salt

about 4 cups all-purpose flour or
  3 1/2 cups bread flour

cornmeal for sprinkling

1. In large bowl, combine 1/4 cup warm water, yeast, and sugar; stir to dissolve. Let stand until foamy, about 5 minutes.

2. With wooden spoon, stir in remaining 1 cup warm water, oil, salt and 1 1/2 cups flour until smooth. Gradually add 2 cups all-purpose flour or 1 1/2 cups bread flour, stirring until dough comes away from side of bowl.

3. Turn dough onto lightly floured surface and knead until smooth and elastic, about 10 minutes, working in enough of remaining 1/2 cup flour just to keep dough from sticking. Shape dough into ball; place in greased large bowl, turning dough to grease top. Cover bowl with plastic wrap and let rise in warm place (80° to 85°F) until doubled in volume, about 1 hour.

4. Punch down dough. Turn onto lightly floured surface and cut in half; cover and let rest 15 minutes. Or, if not using right away, place dough in greased large bowl, cover loosely with greased plastic wrap, and refrigerate up to 24 hours.

5. Sprinkle two large cookie sheets with cornmeal. Shape each dough half into ball. On one prepared cookie sheet, with floured rolling pin, roll one ball into 14" by 10" rectangle. Fold edges to form 1-inch rim. Repeat to make second pizza.

EACH 1/8 DOUGH About 262 calories | 7g protein | 49g carbohydrate | 4g total fat (1g saturated) | 0mg cholesterol | 584mg sodium.

Quick Pizza Dough

In twenty-five minutes, this dough is ready to be turned into a fabulous pizza.

PREP 25 minutes **BAKE** 15 minutes **MAKES** enough dough for 1 large pizza, 2 medium pizzas, or 4 small pizzas; 4 main-dish servings.

about 2 cups all-purpose flour

1 package quick-rise yeast

3/4 teaspoon salt

3/4 cup very warm water
 (120° to 130°F)

cornmeal for sprinkling

1. In large bowl, combine 2 cups flour, yeast, and salt. Stir in very warm water until blended and dough comes away from side of bowl. Turn onto lightly floured surface; knead until smooth and elastic, about 5 minutes.

2. Shape dough into one ball for one large rectangular pizza, two balls for two 10-inch round pizzas, or four balls for four 6-inch round pizzas. Place on cookie sheet (for four balls, use two cookie sheets). Cover loosely with greased plastic wrap; let rest 10 minutes.

3. Sprinkle large cookie sheet with cornmeal. Shape dough: To make one large pizza, on prepared cookie sheet, roll dough into 14^1/$_2$" by 10^1/$_2$" rectangle; fold edges in to form 1-inch rim. For two 10-inch pizzas, pat and stretch one ball into 10-inch round. Form 1-inch rim. Repeat to make second pizza. For four 6-inch pizzas, pat and stretch one ball into 6-inch round. Form ^{1}/$_2$-inch rim. Repeat to make three more pizzas.

EACH 1/4 **DOUGH** About 233 calories | 7g protein | 48g carbohydrate | 1g total fat (0g Saturated) | 0mg cholesterol | 438 mg sodium.

Cheese Pizza

Homemade pizza is surprisingly easy to make. If you like, sprinkle the top with one teaspoon dried oregano or two to three tablespoons chopped fresh basil just before serving.

PREP 20 minutes plus rising **BAKE** 15 minutes **MAKES** 4 main-dish servings.

Basic Pizza Dough (page 113) or Quick Pizza Dough (page 114)

1 cup Pizza Sauce (page 116)

cornmeal

2 tablespoons freshly grated Parmesan cheese

2 cups shredded mozzarella cheese

1. Prepare pizza dough and pizza sauce. (If using Basic Pizza Dough, reserve half of dough for separate pizza.)

2. Shape pizza dough as directed. Sprinkle with Parmesan. Spread pizza sauce over Parmesan and top with mozzarella. Let rest 20 minutes.

3. Meanwhile, preheat oven to 450°F. Bake pizza until crust is golden, 15 to 20 minutes.

EACH SERVING About 391 calories | 14g protein | 55g carbohydrate | 12g total fat (5g saturated) | 25mg cholesterol | 900mg sodium.

Pizza Sauce

Here's a recipe for a zesty pizza sauce that's ready in just minutes.

PREP 12 minutes **COOK** 20 minutes **MAKES** 3 cups.

1 tablespoon olive oil

1 large garlic clove,
   finely chopped

1 can (28 ounces) tomatoes in
   thick puree, chopped

1/4 teaspoon salt

In nonreactive 2-quart saucepan, heat oil over medium heat. Stir in garlic and cook, stirring frequently, until golden, about 30 seconds. Add tomatoes with their puree and salt; heat to boiling over high heat. Reduce heat and simmer 10 minutes.

EACH SERVING About 28 calories | 1g protein | 4g carbohydrate | 11g total fat (0g saturated) | 0mg cholesterol | 153mg sodium.

More Pizza Toppings

Here are more delicious ideas for your pizzas. To keep the crust crispy, scatter cheese over the dough before topping with vegetables and other ingredients. Sprinkle fresh herbs over the pizza just before serving.

- Grilled radicchio, cooked crumbled pancetta or bacon, crumbled goat cheese, chopped fresh sage.

- Sautéed cremini mushrooms, cooked sweet Italian sausage, thinly sliced fresh mozzarella cheese, dried oregano.

- Coarsely chopped grilled eggplant, marinated artichoke hearts, chopped plum tomatoes, shredded mozzarella cheese, fresh basil leaves.

Grilled Pizza

Grilling gives pizza a crisp crust and great smoky flavor. Let the coals burn down until medium-hot, or the crust might scorch.

PREP 35 minutes plus rising   **GRILL** 10 minutes   **MAKES** 4 main-dish servings.

Basic Pizza Dough (page 113) or Quick Pizza Dough (page 114)

2 tablespoons olive oil

8 ounces fresh mozzarella cheese, thinly sliced

12 basil leaves

2 medium tomatoes (6 ounces each), thinly sliced

salt

ground black pepper

1. Prepare pizza dough (if using Basic Pizza Dough, reserve half of dough for separate pizza). Prepare grill.

2. Shape dough into two 10-inch rounds or four 6-inch rounds (do not form rims). Place dough rounds on grill rack over medium heat; grill until underside of dough turns golden and grill marks appear, 2 to 5 minutes.

3. With tongs, turn crusts over. Brush lightly with some oil. Arrange mozzarella on crust, then top with basil and tomatoes. Grill until cheese begins to melt, 3 to 5 minutes longer. Drizzle with remaining oil and sprinkle with salt and pepper.

EACH SERVING About 500 calories | 17g protein | 54g carbohydrate | 23g total fat (1g saturated) | 40mg cholesterol | 629mg sodium.

GH Test Kitchen Tip

Instead of homemade dough you can use 1 pound of frozen bread dough, or 2 packages (10 ounces each) refrigerated pizza dough (found in the dairy case of your supermarket).

Panettone

Tall, domed loaves of panettone are often given as Christmas gifts. Commercially made versions of this festive bread are widely available—which makes homemade panettone all the more special. Beat the dough by hand or use a heavy-duty stand mixer.

PREP 35 minutes   **GRILL** 30 minutes   **MAKES** 2 loaves, 8 wedges each.

$1/2$ cup milk, heated to lukewarm (105° to 115°F)

1 package active dry yeast

$3 1/4$ cups all-purpose flour

$1/2$ cup butter or margarine (1 stick), softened

$1/2$ cup sugar

1 tablespoon freshly grated orange peel

$1 1/2$ teaspoons vanilla extract

$1/2$ teaspoon salt

3 large eggs

$1/2$ cup golden raisins

$1/3$ cup chopped candied lemon peel

vegetable shortening for greasing coffee cans

1. In medium bowl, combine warm milk, yeast, and $1/2$ cup flour. Cover bowl and let stand 45 minutes. (Mixture will bubble and rise.)

2. In bowl of heavy-duty stand mixer, with mixer at medium speed, beat butter, sugar, orange peel, vanilla, and salt until light and fluffy. Alternately beat in eggs and remaining $2 3/4$ cups flour until well combined. Beat in yeast mixture. Stir in raisins and candied lemon peel. Place dough in greased large bowl, turning dough over to grease top. Cover bowl and let rise in warm place (80° to 85°F) until doubled, about 2 hours.

3. Meanwhile, brush insides of two clean $11 1/2$-ounce coffee cans with shortening. Punch down dough and divide between 2 cans. Cover cans and let rise in warm place until dough has doubled and risen almost to top of cans, 1 hour 15 minutes to 2 hours.

4. Preheat oven to 350°F. Bake breads about 30 to 35 minutes, until golden brown and skewer inserted in center of each loaf comes out clean. Remove from cans to cool on wire rack. To serve, cut into wedges.

EACH SERVING About 225 calories | 4g protein | 33g carbohydrate | 9g total fat (4g saturated) | 56mg cholesterol | 150mg sodium.

Fresh Mozzarella and Tomato Sandwiches

The essence of summer—with garden tomatoes and creamy fresh mozzarella. Our parsley-caper sauce makes a terrific spread for grilled meats and fish, too.

PREP 15 minutes **MAKES** 4 main-dish servings.

$^1/_2$ **cup Salsa Verde (below)**

1 large round or oval loaf Tuscan bread

2 ripe medium tomatoes, each cut into 4 slices

8 ounces fresh mozzarella cheese, cut into 8 slices

1. Prepare Salsa Verde.

2. Cut eight $^1/_2$-inch thick slices from center of bread. Spread about 1 tablespoon salsa verde on one side of each bread slice. Place 2 tomato slices and 2 mozzarella slices on each of 4 bread slices. Place remaining bread slices, sauce side down, on top. Cut sandwiches in half.

EACH SERVING About 455 calories | 17g protein | 38g carbohydrate | 26g total fat (9g saturated) | 44mg cholesterol | 690mg sodium.

Salsa Verde

In food processor with knife blade attached or in blender, combine **1 garlic clove,** cut in half, **2 cups packed fresh Italian parsley leaves** (about 3 bunches), $^1/_3$ **cup olive oil, 3 tablespoons capers,** drained, **3 tablespoons fresh lemon juice, 1 teaspoon Dijon mustard,** $^1/_4$ **teaspoon salt,** $^1/_8$ **teaspoon coarsely ground black pepper** and process until finely chopped. If not using sauce right away, cover and refrigerate up to 3 days. Makes about $^3/_4$ cup.

EACH TABLESPOON About 60 calories | 0g protein | 1g carbohydrate | 6g total fat (1g saturated) | 0mg cholesterol | 140mg sodium.

Mozzarella in Carrozza

Mozzarella in carrozza, "mozzarella in a carriage," is usually deep-fried, but we panfry ours. It is served with a buttery anchovy sauce, which can be drizzled over each serving.

PREP 20 minutes **COOK** 5 minutes **MAKES** 8 appetizer servings.

8 ounces part-skim mozzarella cheese

8 slices firm white bread, crusts removed

2 large eggs, well beaten

$1/4$ cup milk

$1/4$ cup all-purpose flour

$1/2$ teaspoon salt

$1/4$ teaspoon ground black pepper

$1/2$ cup plain dried bread crumbs

3 tablespoons vegetable oil

4 tablespoons butter or margarine

8 anchovy fillets, drained

1 tablespoon chopped fresh parsley

1 teaspoon capers, drained

1 teaspoon fresh lemon juice

1. Stand mozzarella on its side and cut lengthwise into 4 equal slices. Place 1 slice cheese between 2 slices bread to form sandwich. Repeat with remaining cheese and bread.

2. Preheat oven to 200°F. In pie plate, with wire whisk, beat eggs and milk. On waxed paper, combine flour, salt, and pepper; spread bread crumbs on separate sheet of waxed paper. Dip sandwiches, one at a time, in flour mixture, shaking off excess, then in egg mixture, and finally in bread crumbs, shaking off excess.

3. In nonstick 12-inch skillet, heat oil over medium heat until hot. Add sandwiches; cook until golden brown, about $1^{1}/_{2}$ minutes per side. Cut each sandwich on diagonal in half. Arrange on platter in single layer. Keep warm in oven.

4. In same skillet, melt butter; add anchovies and cook, stirring constantly, 1 minute. Add parsley, capers, and lemon juice; cook 30 seconds longer. Transfer sauce to small bowl. Serve sauce with sandwiches.

EACH SERVING About 309 calories | 13g protein | 22g carbohydrate | 19g total fat (8g saturated) | 89mg cholesterol | 713mg sodium.

Sausage Calzones

A pizza-parlor specialty, these half-moon turnovers are stuffed with a "three-cheese-plus" filling. Served hot from the oven, with a salad alongside, calzones make an excellent supper.

PREP 45 minutes plus rising   **BAKE** 30 to 35 minutes   **MAKES** 6 main-dish servings.

Basic Pizza Dough (Page 113)

8 ounces sweet or hot Italian sausage links, casings removed

1 small onion, finely chopped

1 garlic clove, finely chopped

1 container (15 ounces) part-skim ricotta cheese

2 ounces part-skim mozzarella cheese, shredded ($^1/_2$ cup)

$^1/_3$ cup freshly grated Parmesan cheese

$^1/_8$ teaspoon ground black pepper

cornmeal

1 tablespoon olive oil

1. Prepare Basic Pizza Dough as directed through Step 3.

2. While dough is rising, prepare filling: In 10-inch skillet, cook sausage, onion, and garlic over medium heat, stirring to break up sausage, about 8 minutes, or until browned. With slotted spoon, transfer sausage mixture to large bowl. Stir in ricotta, mozzarella, Parmesan, and pepper until blended.

3. Preheat oven to 450°F. Sprinkle large cookie sheet with cornmeal.

4. Divide dough into 6 equal pieces. On lightly floured surface, with floured rolling pin, roll each piece of dough into 6-inch round. Spoon about 2/3 cup filling onto half of each round, leaving $^1/_2$-inch border. Fold uncovered half over filling and pinch edges together firmly. With back of fork, press edges to seal. Brush with oil. Repeat with remaining dough, filling, and oil.

5. Place turnovers on prepared cookie sheet on bottom rack in oven. Bake 30 to 35 minutes, until golden. Transfer to wire rack and let cool 5 minutes before serving.

EACH SERVING About 670 calories | 28g protein | 77g carbohydrate | 27g total fat (10g saturated) | 57mg cholesterol | 1,280mg sodium.

Desserts

Lemon-Ricotta Cheesecake
recipe on page 129

Sweet Plum Cassata

Don't be put off by the timing of this recipe: You have to make it a day ahead so it can firm up enough to slice easily, but that frees up plenty of time to prepare the rest of the meal.

PREP 35 minutes plus overnight to chill **COOK** 15 minutes **MAKES** 10 servings.

2 large navel oranges

1 tablespoon margarine or butter

1 1/2 pounds ripe purple plums, coarsely chopped

1/3 cup packed light brown sugar

1 container (15 ounces) whole-milk ricotta

1/2 teaspoon vanilla extract

1/4 teaspoon ground cinnamon

1/2 cup confectioners' sugar

4 teaspoons granulated sugar

1 frozen pound cake (10³/4 ounces), cut into 20 thin slices

raspberries and mint sprig (optional)

1. From oranges, grate 1/2 teaspoon peel and squeeze 3/4 cup juice. In 10-inch skillet, melt margarine over medium heat. Add plums and brown sugar and cook, stirring frequently, until plums are tender, about 5 minutes. Stir in 1/4 cup orange juice. Increase heat to high and cook until plums are very tender, 7 to 8 minutes longer. Cool to room temperature.

2. Meanwhile, in food processor with knife blade attached, blend ricotta until smooth (or press ricotta through fine-meshed sieve over medium bowl). Stir in orange peel, vanilla, cinnamon, and confectioners' sugar. Cover and refrigerate until ready to use.

3. In 1-quart saucepan, heat granulated sugar and remaining 1/2 cup orange juice to boiling over medium heat; cook 1 minute. Cool orange syrup to room temperature.

4. Line 8¹/2" by 4¹/2" loaf pan with plastic wrap, leaving a 4-inch overhang. Arrange 5 slices pound cake, slightly overlapping, on bottom of loaf pan. Brush each slice with orange syrup before topping with next slice. Spread half of ricotta mixture over cake slices. Top with 5 more slices pound cake, brushing with syrup and overlapping slightly; spread with plum mixture. Top with 5 slices pound cake, brushing with syrup and overlapping slightly; spread with remaining ricotta. Top with remaining pound cake slices, brushing with syrup and overlapping as before. Fold plastic wrap over to cover completely. Refrigerate overnight.

5. To serve, open plastic wrap. Invert cake onto long platter. Lift off loaf pan and plastic wrap. Garnish with raspberries and mint sprig, if you like.

EACH SERVING About 300 calories | 6g protein | 40g carbohydrate | 14g total fat (5g saturated) | 21mg cholesterol | 145mg sodium.

Cannoli Cake Roll

This festive cake has a creamy ricotta and cream cheese filling.

PREP I hour 30 minutes plus cooling and chilling BAKE 10 minutes   Makes 14 servings.

CAKE

5 large eggs, separated

1/2 cup granulated sugar

I teaspoon vanilla extract

1/2 cup all-purpose flour

2 tablespoons orange-flavored
   liqueur

I tablespoon water

I tablespoon granulated sugar

confectioners' sugar

RICOTTA FILLING

1 1/4 cups ricotta cheese

4 ounces Neufchâtel

1/2 cup confectioners' sugar

1/2 teaspoon vanilla extract

1/4 teaspoon ground cinnamon

1/4 cup semisweet chocolate
   mini-chips

FROSTING

3/4 cup heavy or whipping cream

3 tablespoons confectioners' sugar

2 tablespoons orange-flavored
   liqueur

1/2 teaspoon vanilla extract

1/4 cup pistachio nuts, chopped

I tablespoon semisweet chocolate
   mini-chips

1. Prepare cake: preheat oven to 350° F. Grease 15 1/2" by 10 1/2" jelly-roll pan. Line with waxed paper; grease paper.

2. In large bowl, with mixer at high speed, beat egg whites until soft peaks form when beaters are lifted. Sprinkle in 1/4 cup granulated sugar, 1 teaspoon at a time, beating until egg whites stand in stiff, glossy peaks when beaters are lifted. Do not overbeat.

3. In small bowl, with mixer at high speed, beat egg yolks, remaining 1/4 cup granulated sugar, and vanilla until very thick and lemon colored, 8 to 10 minutes. Reduce speed to low; stir in flour until blended. With rubber spatula, gently fold egg-yolk mixture into beaten egg whites just until blended.

4. Evenly spread batter in prepared pan. Bake until cake springs back when lightly pressed, 10 to 15 minutes.

5. Meanwhile, in cup, stir orange liqueur, water, and granulated sugar until sugar has dissolved.

6. Sift confectioners' sugar onto clean kitchen towel. When cake is done, run thin knife around edges of cake to loosen from sides of pan; invert onto towel. Carefully remove waxed paper. Brush cake with orange-liqueur mixture. From a long side, roll cake up with towel jelly-roll fashion. Place rolled cake, seam side down, on wire rack; cool completely.

7. Meanwhile, prepare ricotta filling: In food processor with knife blade attached, process ricotta, Neufchâtel, confectioners' sugar, vanilla, and cinnamon until smooth. Transfer filling to bowl; stir in chocolate chips. Cover and refrigerate filling while cake cools.

8. Gently unroll cooled cake. With narrow metal spatula, spread ricotta filling over cake, leaving $1/2$-inch border. Starting from same long side, roll cake up (without towel). Place rolled cake, seam side down, on platter.

9. Prepare frosting: In small bowl, with mixer at medium speed, beat cream and confectioners' sugar until soft peaks form. With rubber spatula, fold in orange liqueur and vanilla. Spread whipped-cream frosting over cake. Refrigerate at least 2 hours or up to 6 hours before serving. Evenly sprinkle top of cake with pistachios and chocolate chips just before serving.

EACH SERVING About 252 calories | 7g protein | 24g carbohydrate | 14g total fat (7g saturated) | 110mg cholesterol | 81mg sodium.

Tiramisù

This classic sweet is a favorite afternoon treat in Italy; literally, it means "pick me up."

PREP 35 minutes plus chilling   MAKES 12 servings.

1 cup hot espresso or very strong brewed coffee

3 tablespoons brandy

2 tablespoons plus $^1/_2$ cup sugar

18 crisp Italian ladyfingers (savoiardi; 5 ounces)

$^1/_2$ cup milk

1 container (16 to 17$^1/_2$ ounces) mascarpone cheese

$^3/_4$ cup heavy or whipping cream

Chocolate Curls (page 140)

unsweetened cocoa

1. In 9-inch pie plate, stir espresso, brandy, and 2 tablespoons sugar until sugar has dissolved; cool to room temperature. Dip both sides of 9 ladyfingers into coffee mixture, one at a time, to soak completely; arrange in single layer in 8-inch square baking dish.

2. In large bowl, stir milk and remaining $^1/_2$ cup sugar until sugar has dissolved. Stir in mascarpone until blended.

3. In small bowl, with mixer at high speed, beat cream until soft peaks form. With rubber spatula, gently fold whipped cream into mascarpone mixture until blended. Spread half of mixture over ladyfingers in baking dish.

4. Dip remaining 9 ladyfingers into coffee mixture and arrange on top of mascarpone mixture. Spread with remaining mascarpone mixture. Refrigerate 3 hours or up to overnight.

5. Meanwhile, prepare Chocolate Curls.

6. Just before serving, dust with cocoa. Cut into squares and spoon into goblets or dessert dishes. Garnish with chocolate curls.

EACH SERVING About 323 calories | 4g protein | 22g carbohydrate | 23g total fat (15g saturated) | 55mg cholesterol | 59mg sodium.

Lemon-Ricotta Cheesecake

This lemony cheesecake has a lighter texture than most (photo on page 123).

PREP 20 minutes plus cooling and chilling   BAKE 1 hour 25 minutes plus standing
MAKES 16 servings.

4 large lemons

1 cup vanilla-wafer crumbs
(about 30 cookies)

4 tablespoons butter or margarine,
melted

1 1/4 cups sugar

1/4 cup cornstarch

2 packages (8 ounces each) cream
cheese, softened

1 container (15 ounces) ricotta
cheese

4 large eggs

2 cups half-and-half or light cream

2 teaspoons vanilla extract

1. Preheat oven to 375°F. From lemons, grate 4 teaspoons peel and squeeze 1/3 cup juice. In 9" by 3" springform pan, combine cookie crumbs, melted butter, and 1 teaspoon lemon peel; stir with fork until evenly moistened. Press mixture firmly onto bottom of pan. Tightly wrap outside of pan with heavy-duty foil. Bake until crust is deep golden, about 10 minutes. Cool completely in pan on wire rack.

2. Turn oven control to 325°F. In small bowl, stir sugar and cornstarch until blended. In large bowl, with mixer at medium speed, beat cream cheese and ricotta until very smooth, about 5 minutes; slowly beat in sugar mixture. Reduce speed to low; beat in eggs, half-and-half, lemon juice, vanilla, and remaining 3 teaspoons lemon peel just until blended, frequently scraping bowl with rubber spatula.

3. Scrape cream-cheese mixture onto crust. Bake 1 hour 15 minutes. Turn off oven; let cheesecake remain in oven 1 hour longer. Remove from oven and transfer to wire rack; remove foil. Run thin knife around edge of cheesecake to prevent cracking during cooling. Cool completely in pan on wire rack. Cover and refrigerate cheesecake until well chilled, at least 6 hours or up to overnight. Remove side of pan to serve.

EACH SERVING About 324 calories | 8g protein | 25g carbohydrate |
22g total fat (13g saturated) | 117mg cholesterol | 182mg sodium.

Caramelized Apple Crostata

A *crostata*, a sweet Italian tart, is often filled with a thin layer of jam, but we made ours with a sautéed apple filling and topped it with a diamond lattice.

PREP I hour 20 minutes plus cooling BAKE I hour MAKES 12 servings.

APPLE FILLING

3 tablespoons butter

2¹/₂ pounds Granny Smith apples (about 5 large), peeled, cored, and cut into ¹/₄-inch-thick slices

¹/₃ cup packed light brown sugar

¹/₄ cup water

COOKIE CRUST

I cup butter (2 sticks), softened (no substitutions)

¹/₂ cup granulated sugar

I large egg plus I large egg yolk

I tablespoon vanilla extract

3 cups all-purpose flour

¹/₄ teaspoon salt

I tablespoon water

1. Prepare filling: In nonstick 12-inch skillet, melt butter over medium heat. Add apples, brown sugar, and water and cook, stirring occasionally, until apples are lightly browned and tender, 20 to 25 minutes. Transfer apples to pie plate; refrigerate until chilled, about 30 minutes.

2. Meanwhile, prepare crust: Preheat oven to 375°F. In large bowl, with mixer at low speed, beat butter and granulated sugar until blended. Increase speed to high; beat until light and creamy, occasionally scraping bowl with rubber spatula. Reduce speed to medium; beat in whole egg and vanilla. With wooden spoon, stir in flour and salt until mixture is crumbly. Press mixture together in bowl and knead a few times until flour is evenly moistened. Shape dough into two disks, one slightly larger than the other. Wrap smaller disk in plastic wrap and refrigerate 30 minutes.

3. Meanwhile, press larger disk of dough onto bottom and halfway up side of 11-inch round tart pan with removable bottom. Wrap tart shell in plastic wrap and refrigerate.

4. On lightly floured waxed paper, roll remaining disk of dough into 12-inch round. With pastry wheel or knife, cut dough into twelve 1-inch-wide strips. Place on a cookie sheet and refrigerate 15 minutes.

5. Spoon chilled filling into tart shell to $1/2$ inch from edge. Place 5 strips, 1 inch apart, across top of tart. Place remaining 5 strips at right angle to first strips to make lattice pattern. Trim ends of strips even with edge of tart and press ends to seal.

6. With hands, roll any dough trimmings and remaining strips into $1/4$-inch-thick ropes. Press ropes around edge of tart to make finished edge. (If ropes break, press pieces together.)

7. In cup, beat egg yolk and water. Brush egg-yolk mixture over lattice and edge of tart.

8. Bake tart until crust is golden, about 1 hour. To prevent overbrowning, cover tart loosely with foil during last 15 minutes of baking. Cool tart in pan on wire rack. When cool, carefully remove side of pan.

EACH SERVING About 385 calories | 4g protein | 50g carbohydrate | 19g total fat (12g saturated) | 84mg cholesterol | 235mg sodium.

Rustic Apricot Crostata

Butter is essential to the texture and flavor; we don't recommend substituting margarine.

PREP 45 minutes plus chilling and cooling **BAKE** 40 minutes **MAKES** 12 servings.

^{1}/$_2$ cup blanched almonds, toasted

3 tablespoons cornstarch

2^1/$_2$ cups all-purpose flour

^{1}/$_4$ teaspoon salt

1 cup butter (2 sticks), softened

^{1}/$_2$ cup plus 2 teaspoons sugar

1 large egg plus 1 large egg yolk

2 teaspoons vanilla extract

1 jar (12 ounces) apricot preserves (about 1 cup)

1 tablespoon water

1. In food processor with knife blade attached, or in blender at high speed, process toasted almonds and cornstarch until finely ground.

2. In medium bowl, combine nut mixture, flour, and salt.

3. In large bowl, with mixer at high speed, beat butter and ^{1}/$_2$ cup sugar until creamy. Add whole egg and vanilla; beat until almost combined (mixture will look curdled). With spoon, stir in flour mixture until dough begins to form. With hands, press dough together. Shape dough into two disks, one slightly larger than the other. Wrap each disk in plastic wrap and refrigerate until dough is firm enough to roll, 1^1/$_2$ to 2 hours.

4. Preheat oven to 375°F. Remove both disks of dough from refrigerator. On lightly floured surface, roll larger disk of dough into 11-inch round. Press dough into bottom and up side of 11-inch round tart pan with removable bottom.

5. On lightly floured waxed paper, roll remaining disk of dough into 12-inch round. With pastry wheel or knife, cut dough into twelve 1-inch-wide strips. Place on cookie sheet and refrigerate 15 minutes.

6. Spread apricot preserves over bottom of tart shell to ^{1}/$_2$ inch from edge. Place 5 strips, 1 inch apart, across top of tart. Place remaining 5 strips at right angle to first strips, to make lattice pattern. Trim ends of strips even with edge of tart and press ends to seal.

7. With hands, roll any dough trimmings and remaining strips into ¹/₄-inch-thick ropes. Press ropes around edge of tart to make finished edge. (If ropes break, press pieces together.)

8. In cup, beat egg yolk and water. Brush egg-yolk mixture over lattice and edge of tart; sprinkle with remaining 2 teaspoons sugar.

9. Bake tart until crust is deep golden, 40 to 45 minutes. If crust puffs up during baking (check occasionally during first 30 minutes), gently press it down with back of spoon. Transfer tart to wire rack to cool completely.

EACH SERVING About 395 calories | 5g protein | 52g carbohydrate | 19g total fat (10g saturated) | 76mg cholesterol | 210mg sodium.

Triple Berry Tart

You can make the filling and crust a day ahead. Just fold in the whipped cream and top with berries when ready to serve.

PREP 30 minutes plus chilling   BAKE 20 minutes   MAKES 12 servings.

**Pastry for 11-Inch Tart
    (page 135)**

1/3 cup sugar

2 tablespoons cornstarch

3 large egg yolks

1 cup milk

**2 tablespoons butter or margarine,
    cut into pieces**

1 teaspoon vanilla extract

1/2 cup heavy or whipping cream

2 cups blueberries (about 1 pint)

2 cups raspberries (about 1 pint)

2 cups blackberries (about 1 pint)

confectioners' sugar

1. Prepare pastry dough as directed through chilling.

2. In small bowl, with wire whisk, combine granulated sugar and cornstarch until blended. Add egg yolks and stir. In 2-quart saucepan, heat milk to simmering over medium-high heat. While beating constantly with wire whisk, gradually pour about half of simmering milk into egg-yolk mixture. Return egg-yolk mixture to saucepan and cook, whisking constantly, until pastry cream has thickened and boils; reduce heat and simmer, stirring, 1 minute. Remove from heat; stir in butter and vanilla until butter has melted. Transfer pastry cream to medium bowl; press plastic wrap onto surface. Refrigerate until well chilled, at least 2 hours or up to 6 hours.

3. Preheat oven to 425°F. Use dough to line 11-inch tart pan with removable bottom. Refrigerate or freeze 10 to 15 minutes to firm dough.

4. Line tart shell with foil; fill with pie weights or dry beans. Bake 15 minutes. Remove foil with weights; bake until golden, 5 to 10 minutes longer. If shell puffs up during baking, gently press it down with back of spoon. Cool completely in pan on wire rack.

5. Up to 2 hours before serving, in small bowl, with mixer at medium speed, beat cream until stiff peaks form. Whisk pastry cream until smooth;

gently fold in whipped cream until blended. Spoon pastry-cream filling into tart shell. In large bowl, gently toss blueberries, raspberries, and blackberries. Spoon over filling and dust with confectioners' sugar.

EACH SERVING About 290 calories | 4 g protein | 30 g carbohydrate | 18 g total fat (10 g saturated) | 95 mg cholesterol | 212 mg sodium.

Pastry for 11-Inch Tart

Tart pastry is a bit richer than pie pastry and bakes up crisper.

PREP 15 minutes plus chilling **MAKES** enough pastry for one 11-inch tart shell.

1¹/₂ cups all-purpose flour

¹/₂ teaspoon salt

¹/₂ cup cold butter or margarine
   (1 stick), cut into pieces

2 tablespoons vegetable shortening

3 to 4 tablespoons ice water

1. In large bowl, combine flour and salt. With pastry blender or two knives used scissor-fashion, cut in butter and shortening until mixture resembles coarse crumbs.

2. Sprinkle in ice water, 1 tablespoon at a time, mixing lightly with fork after each addition, until dough is just moist enough to hold together.

3. Shape dough into disk; wrap in plastic wrap. Refrigerate 30 minutes or up to overnight. (If chilled overnight, let stand 30 minutes at room temperature before rolling.)

4. On lightly floured surface, with floured rolling pin, roll dough into 14-inch round. Ease dough into 11-inch tart pan with removable bottom. Fold overhang in and press dough against side of pan so it extends ¹/₈ inch above rim. Refrigerate or freeze until firm, 10 to 15 minutes. Fill and bake as directed in recipe.

EACH ¹/₁₂th PASTRY About 148 calories | 2g protein | 13g carbohydrate | 10g total fat (5g saturated) | 21mg cholesterol | 175mg sodium.

Panna Cotta with Raspberry Sauce

Panna cotta **means "cooked cream" even though it is barely cooked at all. Try the versatile raspberry sauce on slices of angel food cake or scoops of ice cream.**

PREP 20 minutes plus chilling   **COOK** 15 minutes   **MAKES** 8 servings.

I envelope unflavored gelatin	**¹/₄ cup sugar**
I cup milk	**I strip (3" by I") lemon peel**
¹/₂ vanilla bean or I¹/₂ teaspoons vanilla extract	**I cinnamon stick (3 inches)**
	Raspberry Sauce (below)
I³/₄ cups heavy or whipping cream	**fresh raspberries**

1. In 2-cup measuring cup, evenly sprinkle gelatin over milk; let stand 2 minutes to soften gelatin slightly. With knife, cut vanilla bean lengthwise in half; scrape out seeds and reserve.

2. In 1-quart saucepan, combine cream, sugar, lemon peel, cinnamon stick, and vanilla bean halves and seeds (do not add vanilla extract); heat to boiling over high heat, stirring occasionally. Reduce heat and simmer, stirring occasionally, 5 minutes. Stir in milk mixture; cook over low heat, stirring frequently, until gelatin has completely dissolved, 2 to 3 minutes.

3. Discard lemon peel, cinnamon stick, and vanilla bean from cream mixture. (Stir in vanilla extract, if using.) Pour cream mixture into medium bowl set in large bowl of ice water. With rubber spatula, stir mixture until it just begins to set, 10 to 12 minutes. Pour cream mixture into eight 4-ounce ramekins. Place ramekins in jelly-roll pan for easier handling. Cover and refrigerate panna cotta until well chilled and set, 4 hours or up to overnight.

4. Meanwhile, prepare Raspberry Sauce.

5. To unmold panna cotta, run tip of knife around edges. Tap side of each ramekin sharply to break seal. Invert onto plates. Spoon raspberry sauce around each panna cotta and sprinkle with raspberries.

EACH SERVING WITHOUT RASPBERRY SAUCE About 228 calories | **3g protein** | **9g carbohydrate** | **20g total fat (13g saturated)** | **76mg cholesterol** | **37mg sodium.**

Raspberry Sauce

Into nonreactive 2-quart saucepan, with back of spoon, press **1 package (10 ounces) frozen raspberries in syrup,** thawed, through fine sieve; discard seeds. Stir in **2 tablespoons red currant jelly** and **2 teaspoons cornstarch.** Heat to boiling over high heat, stirring constantly; boil 1 minute. Let cool to room temperature, or cover and refrigerate up to 2 days. Makes 1 cup.

EACH TABLESPOON About 26 calories | **0g protein** | **7g carbohydrate** | **0g total fat** | **0mg cholesterol** | **1mg sodium.**

Cappuccino Cream with Warm Chocolate Sauce

You can make this silky dessert, including the sauce, up to two days ahead. Before serving, invert onto plates and drizzle with the semisweet topping. If you like, garnish the desserts with chocolate curls.

PREP 20 minutes plus chilling **COOK** 5 minutes **MAKES** 8 servings.

CAPPUCCINO CREAM

I envelope unflavored gelatin

1/4 cup milk

1 1/4 cups water

3/4 cup finely ground espresso-coffee beans (about 1 cup coffee beans)

I cinnamon stick (3 inches)

1/2 cup sugar

1 3/4 cups heavy or whipping cream

CHOCOLATE SAUCE

2 squares (2 ounces) semisweet chocolate

1/4 cup heavy or whipping cream

Chocolate Curls (optional, page 140)

1. Prepare Cappuccino Cream: In 1-cup measuring cup, evenly sprinkle gelatin over milk; let stand 5 minutes to soften gelatin slightly.

2. In 1-quart saucepan, heat water, ground coffee, and cinnamon stick over high heat, stirring often, just until mixture begins to boil. Remove from heat; cover and let brew 10 minutes.

3. Line sieve with coffee filter or paper towel. Pour coffee mixture through sieve into 2-cup measuring cup; discard cinnamon stick. (You should have about 3/4 cup liquid.)

4. Return brewed coffee to same saucepan. Add gelatin mixture and sugar and heat over medium-low heat, stirring frequently, until gelatin and sugar have completely dissolved, about 1 minute.

5. Pour coffee mixture and cream into medium bowl set in large bowl of ice water. With rubber spatula, stir mixture until it just begins to set, about 20 minutes.

6. Immediately pour cream mixture into eight 4-ounce ramekins or custard cups. Place ramekins in jelly-roll pan for easier handling. Cover and refrigerate until well chilled and set, at least 4 hours or up to overnight.

7. Meanwhile, prepare Chocolate Sauce: In 1-quart saucepan, heat chocolate and cream over low heat, stirring constantly, until chocolate has melted. Remove from heat; cool 5 minutes.

8. To unmold cappuccino cream, warm small knife under hot water; dry. Run tip of knife around edges. Tap side of each ramekin sharply to break seal. Invert onto dessert plates. Spoon warm sauce over each cappuccino cream and garnish with chocolate curls, if using.

EACH SERVING WITHOUT CHOCOLATE CURLS About 295 calories | 3g protein | 20g carbohydrate | 24g total fat (14g saturated) | 83mg cholesterol | 30mg sodium.

Chocolate Curls

Use these curls to garnish ice cream, cakes, and pies.

PREP 15 minutes plus chilling

1 package (6 ounces) semisweet chocolate chips

2 tablespoons vegetable shortening

1. In heavy 1-quart saucepan, combine chocolate chips and shortening; heat over low heat, stirring frequently, until melted and smooth.

2. Pour chocolate mixture into foil-lined or disposable $5^{3}/_{4}$" by $3^{1}/_{4}$" loaf pan. Refrigerate until chocolate has set, about 2 hours.

3. Remove chocolate from pan. Using vegetable peeler and working over waxed paper, draw blade across surface of chocolate to make large curls. If chocolate is too cold and curls break, let chocolate stand at room temperature until slightly softened, about 30 minutes. To avoid breaking curls, use toothpick or wooden skewer to transfer.

Ricotta Pie

Food Director Susan Westmoreland's Aunt Alice used to make this family favorite every holiday—a tradition Westmoreland happily carries on.

PREP 50 minutes plus chilling   **BAKE** 35 minutes   **MAKES** 20 servings.

CRUST

$^3/_4$ cup margarine or butter (1$^1/_2$ sticks), softened

$^1/_3$ cup sugar

1 large egg

2 teaspoons vanilla extract

2 cups all-purpose flour

$^1/_4$ teaspoon salt

RICOTTA FILLING

1 package (8 ounces) cream cheese, softened

$^3/_4$ cup sugar

$^1/_4$ teaspoon ground cinnamon

1 container (32 ounces) ricotta cheese

5 large egg whites, beaten

1. Prepare crust: In large bowl, with mixer at low speed, beat margarine and sugar until blended. Increase speed to high; beat until light and creamy, occasionally scraping bowl with rubber spatula. Reduce speed to medium; beat in egg until blended. Beat in vanilla. With wooden spoon, stir in flour and salt until dough begins to form. With hands, press dough together. Shape dough into a disk and wrap in plastic wrap; refrigerate until dough is firm enough to handle, about 30 minutes.

2. Meanwhile, prepare filling: In large bowl, with mixer at low speed, beat cream cheese, sugar, and cinnamon until blended. Increase speed to high; beat until light and creamy. Reduce speed to medium; add ricotta cheese and all but 1 tablespoon egg whites and beat just until blended. Set aside.

3. Preheat oven to 400°F. Lightly grease 13" by 9" glass baking dish.

4. With floured hands, press dough evenly onto bottom and up sides of baking dish; make decorative edge. Brush remaining egg white over dough. Pour in ricotta mixture; spread evenly.

5. Bake 25 minutes. Reduce heat to 350°F and bake until center barely jiggles, 10 to 15 minutes longer. Cool completely in pan on wire rack. Cover and refrigerate until well chilled, 6 hours or up to overnight.

EACH SERVING About 275 calories | 8g protein | 22g carbohydrate | 17g total fat (8g saturated) | 46mg cholesterol | 210mg sodium.

Angeletti

Freelance home economist Marjorie Cubisino says her mother-in-law, Carmel, is "the best cook I ever met!" Carmel made these Italian cookies every December for the holidays—they have been Marjorie's husband's favorite since he was a child.

PREP 40 minutes plus cooling   **BAKE** 7 minutes per batch   **MAKES** about 60 cookies.

₁/₂ cup butter or margarine (1 stick), melted

³/₄ cup granulated sugar

¹/₄ cup whole milk

1¹/₂ teaspoons vanilla extract

3 large eggs

3 cups all-purpose flour

1 tablespoon baking powder

¹/₄ teaspoon salt

2 cups confectioners' sugar

3 tablespoons plus 1¹/₂ teaspoons water

¹/₂ cup multicolor candy décors

1. Preheat oven to 375°F. Grease large cookie sheet.

2. In large bowl, with wire whisk, beat butter, granulated sugar, milk, vanilla, and eggs until blended. In medium bowl, mix flour, baking powder, and salt. Stir flour mixture into egg mixture until well blended. Press plastic wrap or waxed paper onto surface of dough; let stand 5 minutes.

3. With floured hands, roll dough into 1-inch balls. Place balls, 2 inches apart, on prepared cookie sheet.

4. Bake until puffed and light brown on bottoms, 7 to 8 minutes. With wide spatula, transfer cookies to wire rack to cool completely. Repeat with remaining dough.

5. When cookies have cooled, in small bowl, with wire whisk, stir confectioners' sugar and water until blended. Dip top of each cookie into glaze; transfer to wire racks set over waxed paper. Immediately sprinkle cookies with décors. Allow glaze to set, about 20 minutes. Layer cookies between waxed paper in air-tight container. Store at room temperature up to 3 days or freeze up to 3 months.

EACH COOKIE About 75 calories | 1g protein | 13g carbohydrate | 2g total fat (1g saturated) | 15mg cholesterol | 55mg sodium.

Mostaccioli

Food Director Susan Westmoreland happily recalls a "sea of cookies" spread atop a clean white sheet on her grandparents' bed—the only place large enough to cool the hundreds of *mostaccioli* Grandma Elsie baked for friends and family.

PREP 45 minutes plus cooling BAKE 7 minutes per batch
MAKES about 60 cookies.

COOKIES

2 cups all-purpose flour

$^1/_2$ cup unsweetened cocoa

$1^1/_2$ teaspoons baking powder

1 teaspoon ground cinnamon

$^1/_4$ teaspoon ground cloves

$^1/_4$ teaspoon salt

$^3/_4$ cup granulated sugar

$^1/_2$ cup butter or margarine (1 stick), softened

1 large egg

$^1/_2$ cup whole milk

CHOCOLATE GLAZE

3 tablespoons unsweetened cocoa

$^1/_4$ cup boiling water

$1^1/_4$ cups confectioners' sugar

white candy décors

1. Prepare cookies: Preheat oven to 400°F. In medium bowl, combine flour, cocoa, baking powder, cinnamon, cloves, and salt. In large bowl, with mixer at low speed, beat granulated sugar and butter until blended, occasionally scraping bowl with rubber spatula. Increase speed to high; beat until light and creamy. At low speed, beat in egg. Alternately beat in flour mixture and milk, beginning and ending with flour mixture, just until combined, occasionally scraping bowl.

2. With cocoa-dusted hands, shape dough into 1-inch balls. Place balls, 2 inches apart, on ungreased large cookie sheet. Bake until puffed (they will look dry and slightly cracked), 7 to 9 minutes. Transfer cookies to wire rack to cool. Repeat with remaining dough.

3. When cookies are cool, prepare glaze: In medium bowl, with wire whisk or fork, mix cocoa and boiling water until smooth. Gradually stir in confectioners' sugar and blend well. Dip top of each cookie into glaze. Place

cookies on wire rack set over waxed paper. Immediately sprinkle cookies with décors. Allow glaze to set, about 20 minutes. Layer between waxed paper in airtight container. Store at room temperature up to 3 days, or freeze up to 3 months.

EACH COOKIE About 55 calories | 1g protein | 9g carbohydrate | 2g total fat (1g saturated) | 8mg cholesterol | 40mg sodium.

Chocolate Hazelnut Macaroons

Chocolate plus hazelnuts equals *gianduja*—a flavor you may have encountered in fine Italian chocolates. These macaroons are a chocolate variation of an Italian recipe called *brutti ma buoni* "ugly but good"—a reference to the fact that the cookies are a bit lumpy and irregular in shape, though absolutely delicious.

PREP 30 minutes BAKE 10 minutes per batch MAKES about 30 cookies.

1 cup hazelnuts (filberts)

1 cup sugar

$^1/_4$ cup unsweetened cocoa

1 square (1 ounce) unsweetened
    chocolate, chopped

$^1/_8$ teaspoon salt

2 large egg whites

1 teaspoon vanilla extract

1. Preheat oven to 350°F. Line 2 large cookie sheets with foil.

2. Place hazelnuts in 9" by 9" metal baking pan. Bake until toasted, 15 minutes. Wrap hot hazelnuts in clean kitchen towel. With hands, roll hazelnuts back and forth to remove skins. Cool.

3. In food processor with knife blade attached, process hazelnuts, sugar, cocoa, chocolate, and salt until nuts and chocolate are finely ground. Add egg whites and vanilla and process until blended.

4. Drop dough by rounded teaspoons, using another spoon to release batter, 2 inches apart, on prepared cookie sheets. Bake until tops feel firm when pressed lightly, about 10 minutes, rotating sheets between upper

and lower oven racks halfway through baking. Cool on cookie sheets on wire racks.

5. Repeat with remaining dough.

EACH COOKIE About 60 calories | **1g protein** | **8g carbohydrate** | **3g total fat (1g saturated)** | **0mg cholesterol** | **15mg sodium.**

Italian Tricolors

During the holidays, Food Appliances Director Sharon Franke and her sister, Nancy Lehrer, would purchase an assortment of cookies at their neighborhood bakery. These multicolored Italian treats were always the first to go. Franke thought only a bakery could make them, but we created a version that any home cook can whip up.

PREP 1 hour plus cooling and chilling BAKE 10 minutes MAKES 36 cookies.

1 tube or can (7 to 8 ounces) almond paste, cut into 1-inch pieces

³/₄ cup butter or margarine (1¹/₂ sticks), softened

³/₄ cup sugar

¹/₂ teaspoon almond extract

3 large eggs

1 cup all-purpose flour

¹/₄ teaspoon salt

15 drops red food coloring

15 drops green food coloring

²/₃ cup apricot preserves

3 squares (3 ounces) semisweet chocolate

1 teaspoon vegetable shortening

1. Preheat oven to 350°F. Grease three 8" by 8" metal baking pans. Line bottoms of pans with waxed paper; grease and flour waxed paper.

2. In large bowl, with mixer at medium-high speed, beat almond paste, butter, sugar, and almond extract until well blended (there will be some small lumps of almond paste remaining). Reduce speed to medium; beat in eggs, one at a time, until blended. Reduce speed to low; beat in flour and salt just until combined.

3. Transfer one-third of batter (about 1 rounded cup) to small bowl. Transfer half of remaining batter to another small bowl. (You should have equal amounts of batter in each bowl.) Stir red food coloring into one bowl of batter until evenly blended. Repeat with green food coloring and another bowl of batter, leaving one bowl untinted. (Batters may still have some small lumps of almond paste remaining.)

4. Spoon untinted batter into one pan. With metal spatula (offset if possible), spread batter evenly (layer will be about ¹/₄ inch thick). Repeat with red batter in second pan. Repeat with green batter in remaining pan.

5. Bake until set and toothpick inserted in centers of layers comes out clean, 10 to 12 minutes, rotating pans between upper and lower oven racks halfway through baking.

6. Cool in pans on wire racks 5 minutes. Run tip of knife around sides of pans to loosen layers. Invert layers onto wire racks, leaving waxed paper attached; cool completely.

7. When layers have cooled, press apricot preserves through coarse sieve into small bowl to remove any large pieces of fruit. Remove waxed paper from green layer; invert onto flat plate or small cutting board. Spread with half of apricot preserves. Remove waxed paper from untinted layer; invert onto green layer. Spread with remaining apricot preserves. Remove waxed paper from red layer; invert onto untinted layer.

8. In 1-quart saucepan, heat chocolate and shortening over low heat, stirring frequently, until melted. Spread melted chocolate mixture on top of red layer (not on sides); refrigerate until chocolate is firm, at least 1 hour. If you like, after chocolate has set, cover and refrigerate stacked layers up to 3 days before cutting and serving.

9. To serve, with serrated knife, trim edges (about $1/4$ inch from each side). Cut stacked layers into 6 strips. Cut each strip crosswise into 6 pieces. Place in single layer in waxed paper-lined, airtight container. Refrigerate up to 1 week, or freeze up to 3 months.

EACH COOKIE About 125 calories | 2g protein | 15g carbohydrate | 7g total fat (3g saturated) | 29mg cholesterol | 65mg sodium.

Pignoli Cookies

The secret to success here are Mediterranean or Italian pine nuts, which are torpedo shaped. They have a more delicate flavor than the flatter Chinese pine nuts.

PREP 45 minutes   **BAKE** 10 to 12 minutes per batch   **MAKES** about 24 cookies.

I tube or can (7 to 8 ounces) almond paste, crumbled into large pieces

$^3/_4$ cup confectioners' sugar

I large egg white

I tablespoon plus I teaspoon honey

$^1/_3$ cup pine nuts (pignoli)

I. Preheat oven to 350°F. In food processor with knife blade attached, process crumbled almond paste and confectioners' sugar until mixture resembles fine crumbs.

2. In large bowl, with mixer at low speed, beat almond-paste mixture, egg white, and honey until blended. Increase speed to high; beat until very smooth, about 5 minutes, occasionally scraping bowl with rubber spatula (mixture will be thick).

3. Line large cookie sheet with parchment paper or greased foil. Spoon almond mixture into large decorating bag with large round tip ($^1/_2$-inch-diameter opening). Pipe mixture into $1^1/_4$-inch rounds, 2 inches apart, onto prepared cookie sheet. With moistened fingertip, gently smooth surface of each cookie. Sprinkle with pine nuts; press gently to cover tops of cookies.

4. Bake cookies until golden brown, 10 to 12 minutes. Cool completely on cookie sheet on wire rack. Or, to reuse cookie sheet right away, slide parchment or foil, with cookies attached, onto wire rack and let cookies cool completely on parchment or foil. Line cookie sheet and repeat with remaining almond mixture and pine nuts.

5. When cool, carefully peel cookies off parchment paper or foil. Place cookies in waxed paper–lined airtight container. Store up to 2 weeks at room temperature.

EACH COOKIE About 70 calories | 2g protein | 9g carbohydrate | 3g total fat (0g saturated) | 0mg cholesterol | 5mg sodium.

Almond-Anise Biscotti

Soaking the anise seeds in liqueur softens them and releases their delicious flavor.

PREP 25 minutes plus cooling   BAKE 55 minutes   MAKES about 60 biscotti.

I tablespoon anise seeds, crushed

I tablespoon anisette
  (anise-flavored liqueur)

2 cups all-purpose flour

I cup sugar

I cup whole almonds (4 ounces),
  toasted and coarsely chopped

I teaspoon baking powder

$1/8$ teaspoon salt

3 large eggs

I. Preheat oven to 325°F. Grease large cookie sheet. In medium bowl, combine anise seeds and anisette; let stand 10 minutes.

2. In large bowl, combine flour, sugar, chopped almonds, baking powder, and salt. With wire whisk, beat eggs into anise mixture. With wooden spoon, stir egg mixture into flour mixture until blended. Divide dough in half. On prepared cookie sheet, with floured hands, shape each half into 15-inch log, placing them 3 inches apart (dough will be sticky).

3. Bake until golden and toothpick inserted in center comes out clean, about 40 minutes. Cool 10 minutes on cookie sheet on wire rack, then transfer logs to cutting board. With serrated knife, cut each log crosswise on diagonal into scant $1/2$-inch-thick slices. Place slices, cut side down, on two ungreased cookie sheets. Bake 15 minutes, turning slices over once and rotating cookie sheets between upper and lower oven racks halfway through baking. With spatula, transfer biscotti to wire racks to cool.

EACH BISCOTTI About 46 calories | 1g protein | 7g carbohydrate |
1g total fat (0g saturated) | 11mg cholesterol | 17mg sodium.

Coffee Granita

A Neapolitan tradition. If you like, use decaffeinated espresso.

PREP 10 minutes plus cooling and freezing   **MAKES** about 5 cups or 10 servings.

$^2/_3$ **cup sugar**

2 cups hot espresso coffee

unsweetened whipped cream (optional)

In medium bowl, stir sugar and espresso until sugar has completely dissolved. Pour into 9-inch square metal baking pan; cool. Cover, freeze, and scrape as directed in tip (opposite). Serve granita with whipped cream, if you like.

**EACH SERVING WITHOUT WHIPPED CREAM About 53 calories |
0g protein | 14g carbohydrate | 0g total fat | 0mg cholesterol | 1mg sodium.**

Lemon Granita

This simple, zesty granita has an invigorating tang.

PREP 10 minutes plus cooling and freezing COOK 10 minutes
MAKES about 4 cups or 8 servings.

I cup sugar   4 large lemons

2 cups water

1. In 2-quart saucepan, combine sugar and water; heat to boiling over high heat, stirring until sugar has dissolved. Reduce heat to medium and cook 5 minutes. Set saucepan in bowl of ice water until syrup is cool.

2. Meanwhile, from lemons, grate 2 teaspoons peel and squeeze $3/4$ cup juice.

3. Stir lemon peel and juice into sugar syrup; pour into 9-inch square metal baking pan. Cover, freeze, and scrape as directed in tip below.

EACH SERVING About 103 calories | 0g protein | 27g carbohydrate | 0g total fat | 0mg cholesterol | 1mg sodium.

GH Test Kitchen Tip

Cover and freeze the granita mixture until partially frozen, about 2 hours. Stir with a fork to break up the chunks. Cover and freeze until the mixture is completely frozen, at least 3 hours or up to overnight. To serve, let the granita stand at room temperature until slightly softened, about 15 minutes. Use a metal spoon to scrape across surface of the granita, transferring the ice shards to chilled dessert dishes or wine goblets without packing them.

Tartufo

These chocolate-coated ice-cream balls are intended to resemble truffles (*tartufo* means "truffle" in Italian).

PREP 30 minutes plus freezing **MAKES** 6 servings.

I pint chocolate or vanilla ice cream

2 tablespoons brandy

6 maraschino cherries, stems removed

I cup fine amaretti cookie crumbs (20 cookies)

1 1/2 cups semisweet chocolate chips

4 tablespoons butter or margarine, cut into pieces

2 tablespoons light corn syrup

1. Place ice cream in refrigerator to soften slightly, about 30 minutes. Line small cookie sheet with waxed paper and place in freezer. Meanwhile, in cup, pour brandy over cherries. Place amaretti crumbs on waxed paper.

2. Working quickly, with large ice-cream scoop (1/3 cup), scoop ball of ice cream. With ice cream still in scoop, gently press 1 cherry deep into center of ball; reshape ice cream around cherry. Release ice-cream ball on top of amaretti crumbs and roll to coat well. Place on prepared cookie sheet in freezer. Repeat to make 6 ice-cream balls. Freeze until firm, at least 1 1/2 hours.

3. In medium bowl set over saucepan of simmering water, heat chocolate chips with butter and corn syrup, stirring occasionally, until chocolate and butter have melted and mixture is smooth. Remove pan from heat, but leave bowl in place to keep chocolate warm for easier coating.

4. Remove 1 ice-cream ball from freezer; place in slotted spoon and slip ice-cream ball into melted chocolate, turning quickly to coat thoroughly. Return to cookie sheet. Repeat with remaining ice-cream balls. Freeze until chocolate is firm, about 1 hour. If not serving right away, wrap in foil and freeze up to 1 day.

5. To serve, let tartufo stand at room temperature until slightly softened, about 10 minutes.

EACH SERVING About 476 calories | 5g protein | 59g carbohydrate | 27g total fat (15g saturated) | 36mg cholesterol | 133mg sodium.

Metric Conversion Charts

The recipes that appear in this cookbook use the standard United States method for measuring liquid and dry or solid ingredients (teaspoons, tablespoons, and cups). The information on this chart is provided to help cooks outside the U.S. successfully use these recipes. All equivalents are approximate.

Metric Equivalents for Different Types of Ingredients

A standard cup measure of a dry or solid ingredient will vary in weight depending on the type of ingredient. A standard cup of liquid is the same volume for any type of liquid. Use the following chart when converting standard cup measures to grams (weight) or milliliters (volume).

Standard Cup	Fine Powder (e.g. flour)	Grain (e.g. rice)	Granular (e.g. sugar)	Liquid Solids (e.g. butter)	Liquid (e.g. milk)
1	140 g	150 g	190 g	200 g	240 ml
3/4	105 g	113 g	143 g	150 g	180 ml
2/3	93 g	100 g	125 g	133 g	160 ml
1/2	70 g	75 g	95 g	100 g	120 ml
1/3	47 g	50 g	63 g	67 g	80 ml
1/4	35 g	38 g	48 g	50 g	60 ml
1/8	18 g	19 g	24 g	25 g	30 ml

Useful Equivalents for Liquid Ingredients By Volume

1/4 tsp =					1 ml
1/2 tsp =					2 ml
1 tsp =					5 ml
3 tsp =	1 tbls =		1/2 fl oz =	15 ml
	2 tbls =	1/8 cup =	1 fl oz =	30 ml
	4 tbls =	1/4 cup =	2 fl oz =	60 ml
	5 1/3 tbls =	1/3 cup =	3 fl oz =	80 ml
	8 tbls =	1/2 cup =	4 fl oz =	120 ml
	10 2/3 tbls =	2/3 cup =	5 fl oz =	160 ml
	12 tbls =	3/4 cup =	6 fl oz =	180 ml
	16 tbls =	1 cup =	8 fl oz =	240 ml
	1 pt =	2 cups =	16 fl oz =	480 ml
	1 qt =	4 cups =	32 fl oz =	960 ml
			33 fl oz =	1000 ml = 1 l

Useful Equivalents For Dry Ingredients By Weight

(To convert ounces to grams, multiply the number of ounces by 30.)

1 oz =	1/16 lb =	30 g
4 oz =	1/4 lb =	120 g
8 oz =	1/2 lb =	240 g
12 oz =	3/4 lb =	360 g
16 oz =	1 lb =	480 g

Useful Equivalents for Length

(To convert inches to centimeters, multiply the number of inches by 2.5.)

1 in =		2.5 cm
6 in =	1/2 ft =	15 cm
12 in =	1 ft =	30 cm
36 in =	3 ft = 1 yd =	90 cm
40 in =		100 cm = 1 m

Useful Equivalents for Cooking/Oven Temperatures

	Fahrenheit	Celsius	Gas Mark
Freeze Water	32° F	0° C	
Room Temperature	68° F	20° C	
Boil Water	212° F	100° C	
Bake	325° F	160° C	3
	350° F	180° C	4
	375° F	190° C	5
	400° F	200° C	6
	425° F	220° C	7
	450° F	230° C	8
Broil			Grill

Index